Today Chardock, Tomorrow the World

Foreword by
David Gower

Published by Tony Williams Football Directories

Richard Digance is one of Britain's top television entertainers with his own TV Show for ITV and a BAFTA Nomination for Comedy in 1990.He has written four other books.'Animal Alphabet' which was serialised on BBC Radio,'Another Animal Alphabet',and two novels 'Backwater' and 'Run Out In The Country'.He is an avid football fan,and it was strange to say the least to find out his neighbour in the quiet pastures of Dorset was none other than football commentator Peter Brackley.

Peter is regarded as one of the finest after-dinner speakers in the country.Like Richard he began in BBC Radio and moved to ITV,appearing on 'Saint and Greavesie'.He has commentated on Olympic Games and three World Cups,now commentating exclusively for British Sky Broadcasting.

Well,it all started at the Professional Footballers' Association Dinner,after two rehearsals at Bristol Rovers and Yeovil Town.Richard and Peter combining their varying talents at a dinner is a much talked about occasion.It was on the way to such an event,in Richard's car,the story of Chardock Rangers began to unfold.

It has been a labour of love,a chance to meet up with old mates from the worlds of sport and show business,and has been a cause of much merriment in the garden during the hot days of the late summer.We hope you enjoy reading this book as much as we enjoyed writing it.

We wish to thank our many friends from the worlds of sport and show business who contributed to this book.Without them, we couldn't have finished this book,and without friends like them,we wouldn't have bothered anyway.They are all mates who have reached the greatest of heights in their chosen professions.They are;

Graham Taylor	England Football Team Manager
Lawrie McMenemy	Assistant England Football Team Manager
Jack Charlton OBE	Republic of Ireland Football Team Manager
David Gower	England Cricket Captain
Bryan Robson OBE	England Football Captain
Fred Dinenage	Television Presenter
Tommy Docherty	Scotland Football Team Manager etc.
Gordon Taylor	Chief Executive.Professional Footballers Assoc.
Jack Taylor OBE JP	World Cup Referee
Geoffrey Boycott	England Cricketer
Mike Payne	Athena Cartoonist
Terry Mott FRCR	Royal College of Surgeons
Ron Atkinson	Football Manager
Hale and Pace	Golden Rose of Montreau Award Comedians
Desmond Lynam	Television Sports Presenter
Billy Wright CBE	England Football Captain
Chris Smith	England Cricketer
Robin Smith	England Cricketer
Alan Ball	England Footballer.World Cup 1966
Liam Brady	Republic of Ireland Footballer
Peter Reid	Football Manager.England Footballer
Mark Nicholas	MCC Cricket Captain
David O'Leary	Republic of Ireland Footballer
Tony Gale	Professional Footballer
Jim Smith	Football Manager
David Gunson	Air Traffic Controller
Kevin King	Radio Presenter
Dickie Davies	Television Presenter

West Ham United Footballers.Ian Bishop,Stuart Slater,Tim Braecker, Matthew Rush,Steve Potts,George Parris.

Jimmy Greaves	Television Presenter

David Gower

Dear Mr Millonaire,

I was very pleased to receive your letter, please find enclosed the returned brick. I will naturally repair my study window at my own expense. To be honest, I confess to being astounded and confused that you bestowed this great honour upon me.

The sad truth is that, at a stage in my career (and I use the term loosely) when it seems I am struggling to achieve recognition in my own sport, it is somewhat of a fillip to be asked to fulfil such an important role as to produce a foreward for your new book.

The difficulty in the compiling of this text is not, may I add, helped by the presence of your snotty nosed nephew peering over my shoulder armed with an air rifle and an airfix model of Paul Gascoigne.

Notwithstanding it is an honour to submit this manuscript, especially considering your more than generous offer for me to act as consultant to Chardock Rangers. I am sure my international sport involvement will stand us both in good stead, particularly with regards the plumbing in the dressing rooms.

I also note with interest the name of your overseas player, Nawab of Chardock. We had a Nawab who used to play a decent game of cricket, despite only having one good eye and three good wives. The last I heard of him he lost an election in India, also despite having one good eye. Perhaps he could be the very man to make up for the continued absence, if not abstinence, of your own noble but errant superstar.

You have certainly set your sights high in your ambition to take the not so mighty Chardock Rangers to the top of the European tree, or should I say bush, but I feel confident that with your determination to succeed and your willingness to employ almost the best to achieve a sort of best. I am sure that it shall be only a matter of time before you achieve your goals, if you will pardon the pun.

By the way if your snivveling little nephew does not sling his hook in the next few minutes, he could be on the wrong end of middle and leg, and may I further add that due to my age, I could well be playing for Durham in the next 25 years, so please direct my mail to the North East.

With all best wishes

Yours sincerely

David Gower

PS: Something has just occurred to me, silly though it may sound — you did know I played cricket didn't you? If not, I sincerely trust this does not alter any agreements we have already discussed.

DG

It had been a disappointing year at Chardock Rangers Football Club.Probably the worst ever in the club's history.They had played 31 and lost 31,letting in 207 goals and scoring not a single one in return.However,of the 207 goals,Dinky Bates had always maintained over two hundred were offside,six were sickening deflections and one was a cracker.

For the best part of seventeen years,with more or less the same team,the Dorset club had turned out,giving its all, in league and cup competitions.Yet they had achieved nothing, bar third place in a charity skittles match at the Dog and Duck,the local public house and boardroom of the Rangers.

Two of Chardock's side,strange as it may seem,had gained International honours by representing England........ as members of the Home Guard during the Second World War.

Throughout the length and breadth of our football crazy nation,dozens and dozens of such football clubs exist best they can,struggling through obscurity and adversity towards who can tell.Chardock Rangers were destined for the same dead-end route until a certain Maurice Millionaire moved into the area.His arrival saw the erection of Europe's largest bungalow,with the most wagon-wheels along its front wall.But his arrival caused something to happen,thus justifying a book such as this.

When he arrived in Dorset it seemed things would change in the sleepy backwater.The future of Chardock Rangers, at last,looked promising.To actually win a game,or close to it, after seventeen years,looked possible.

Maurice Millionaire had amassed his small fortune in the respectable world of second hand car dealing,and with his kind offer of eleven sponsored club mopeds,seven with MOT certificates,he was immediately elevated to the heady position of Club Chairman.A strange twist for the man who'd moved to Chardock in a bid to steer clear of the Inland Revenue and Her Majesty's Customs and Excise.He blew his cover in an area of peace and tranquility to lead the assault towards fame and notoriety in the annals of Football history.For this is a story that will be told for many many years to come,long after Ron Atkinson has run out of teams to manage.

Sadly,Maurice knew nothing of the game,yet unperturbed,he instigated a master plan.To create,under the proud banner of Chardock Rangers,the greatest football team in the World. A club which,in years to come,would nestle comfortably amongst the all-time great names of Barcelona,Real Madrid, Red Star Belgrade and Redbridge Forest.

At the time of his appointment to the board,club assets amounted to three players and nowhere to play.A far cry from the European Cup,miles from the UEFA Cup,even the Dorset under 13's Subbuteo Championships.

But,Maurice Millionaire had a dream and even the wildest of dreams can sometimes come true.The following letters of correspondence are sufficient evidence of both his dream and his determination.

Never say die,From little acorns,where there's a will, never kick a dog in the knackers when he's got your hand in his mouth.Clusters of proverbs as much a part of olde England as the rolling hills of Thomas Hardy's Dorset.Yes Hardy no less,himself a keen Arsenal fan,had walked the very contours that sloped down to Chardock as it nodded lazily,from day to day.

For the greatest football team in the World,the finest facilities were necessary.A one hundred thousand seater stadium, the size of Wembley.Five star travel for the finest players in the land.Camp-sites were needed for visiting teams.

So,from the fields of waving barley and corn was to grow the greatest rags to riches story.Or was it?

Were the happy and contented folk of Chardock ready for such an invasion and intrusion?

More to the point,did the people of Chardock really want all this upheaval?

What is the Capital of Chad? And Why?

Such questions were asked and debated throughout the thatched houses and inns,the highways and by-ways around the parish.Maurice Millionaire was a forceful man,used to having his own way through both brute force and ignorance.His use of the English language left a lot to be desired.He thought a verb was something you cooked with and shoved in a rack in the kitchen. His literary skills were beaten on the useless stakes only by his knowledge of our beloved national game.

Can you believe he invited David Gower,one of Britain's most magnificent cricketers to write the foreword for this book,thinking he was an international footballer.The man had no idea and even less shame.

Each letter which follows is authentic,each reply is completely genuine.The famous responded in their varying ways as Maurice Millionaire set about making his dream come true. To many it would have been a nightmare.

The following is a fine account of persistence,front and down right nerve.To build the stadium he needed land,so maybe the estate agents is the right place to begin our story. And so.........

TVS Production
Television Centre
Southampton SO9 5HZ
Telephone: 0703-634211
Fax: 0703-211428
Telex: 477217

TVS

Dear Maurice Millionaire,

So you've going to build the greatest team in the world? How ?!!!!

Good Luck!

Fred Dinenage.

P.S. Play up Pompey!

CHARDOCK RANGERS FOOTBALL CLUB THE ALLOTMENTS,CHARDOCK

The Greatest Football Team in the World

Headed notepaper still on drawing board.

Mr Martin Diplock,
Estate Agent,
Broad Street,
Lyme Regis.

Dear Martin Diplock,

As a local estate agent,I write in the hope you can help in securing me a football stadium in magnolia, somewhere around the size of Wembley,within the parish of Chardock.

Naturally,money is no object,up to £20,000,and the stadium must be detached.A garden is not necessary.Dressing room facilities containing a spring-fed pond for washing,and twenty two bronze hooks for hanging grubby football shirts are essential,as indeed's a shed for the referee.This building mustn't have windows so as adequate bribing can take place with the utmost security.

Could you look into this for me? I look forward to hearing from you.

Maurice Millionaire
Chairman
Chardock Rangers Football Club.

Surveyors and Valuers
Auctioneers and Estate Agents

48 Broad Street
Lyme Regis
Dorset DT7 3QF

Telephone: (02974) 2155

MJD/TC

1.7.91.

Morris Millionaire Esq.,
Chardock Rangers Football Club,
The Allotments,
CHARDOCK,
Dorset.

Dear Mr Millionaire,

Thank you for your recent letter.

Surprising as it may seem, we have no purpose-built football stadiums on our register and are not aware of any that are likely to come onto the market in the next few months.

We do, however have a nice 3 bedroomed bungalow for sale which is painted out in magnolia (your specified colour). This property has a very large garden and (subject to planning approval) the accommodation could be converted to changing rooms with shower facilities and also an executive bathroom. Also, it does have a garden pond which fulfills yet another of your preferences. As I have said, the garden is large but in order to fit in the stands and car parking I think the remaining space would only allow you to have a fairly small pitch - does this really matter, as it will mean less wear and tear on the players?

Another idea I have had is that this town's allotment site may be suitable and it is possible that you could acquire it. This is certainly large enough and to save money one of the many corrugated iron garden sheds on the site would be useful for referee accommodation. The only problem with this site is that it is on the cliff edge and has quite a slope on it, but to a man of your obvious ingenuity this should not prove to be an insurmountable difficulty.

Please let me know if I can be of any further help, or you wish to make an inspection of the above properties.

Yours sincerely,

Martin Diplock

M.J. DIPLOCK, F.R.I.C.S.
ALDER KING

CHARDOCK RANGERS FOOTBALL CLUB,THE ALLOTMENTS,CHARDOCK,DORSET

The Greatest Football Team in the World

Headed notepaper last of my problems.

Bryan Moore,
Club Chairman.
Yeovil Town Football Club,
The Slope,
Yeovil,

Dear Bryan Moore,

How much I enjoyed those hundred or more games when you captained England.What a player.

I'm in the process of knocking up a one hundred thousand seater stadium in Chardock,and the only land up for grabs is a cliff edge,and it therefore slopes.As Yeovil have the most famous slope in the western hemisphere,I was wondering if you'd be prepared to sell it at a modest sum to my club. With luck,it may be the same gradient as my cliff edge,and,if it is,I can turn it round.The two slopes would then cancel each other out and my football pitch would be flat.

What do you think Bobby? I am also led to believe Ian Botham once played for your club.Will he be available to turn out in our colours next season?

I await your reply fellow chairman.

Yours faithfully,

Maurice Millionaire
Chardock Rangers Football Club.

Yeovil Town Football Club

Controlled by the Yeovil Football and Athletic Club Limited
Reg. No. 189754 (England) VAT No. 186 6136 39

Members of the Football Association

Manager's Office, Club Secretary's Office and Registered Offices:

**Huish Park,
Lufton Way,
Yeovil,
Somerset BA22 8YF**

**Telephone: (0935) 23662
(0935) 79777
(Commercial & Lottery Dept)**

Fax: 0935 73956

Restaurant: (0935) 32110

Manager:

General Manager & Secretary:
R. L. BRINSFORD

THE GM VAUXHALL CONFERENCE
Great Mills League
South West Counties League

President:
S. N. BURFIELD, MBE

Chairman:
B. W. MOORE

Vice Chairman:
J. A. HOUGHTON

Directors:

M. SPEARPOINT
A. K. WILLIAMS
G. R. SMITH

Commercial Manager:
A. SKIRTON

Mr Maurice Millionaire,
Chardock Rangers Football Club
The Allotments
Chardock
Dorset

Dear Mr Millionaire,

Thank you for your letter received this morning. Unfortunately we are unable to help as we moved to our new Huish Park stadium a while ago,having sold the old ground with the infamous slope to Tesco super markets.If the slope you wish to buy still exists no-one can tell,but a certain indication will be if the trolleys roll unaided down the aisles of the supermarket upon completion.I would consider this most unlikely and would advise you to search elsewhere for your soil.

I am sorry we can be of little assistance and wish your club the very best of luck in becoming the greatest team in the world.By the way,Ian Botham now plays cricket and I'm sure is very busy at this present time.

Yours sincerely,

Bryan Moore

Bryan Moore
Chairman
Yeovil Town Football Club.

CHARDOCK RANGERS FOOTBALL CLUB,THE ALLOTMENTS,CHARDOCK

The Greatest Football Team in the World

Mr Mike Keep
Managing Director
Manders Paints Decorative Division
PO Box 9
Wolverhampton
The Midlands.

Dear Mike Keep,

I am growing a football pitch for my new club Chardock Rangers.Due to your paint company's involvement with Wolverhampton Wanderers,a great club like ourselves,I thought I'd drop you a line.

Our club require some circular white paint for our centre circle and a tin of semi-circular paint in white for the two penalty areas.Plus of course the necessary undercoat.

We also require two white blobs to use as penalty spots.

I would be interested to know if you could supply these,and how much would it cost? I would also like to open an account with you,so if you could get the girl who deals with the readies to give me a call,I'll sort it out.

Yours faithfully,

Maurice Millionaire
Chardock Rangers Football Club.

Decorative Division

Manders Paints Ltd.
P.O. Box 9, Old Heath Road
Wolverhampton WV1 2XG

Telephone (0902) 871028
Telex 338354
Fax (0902) 452435

Our Ref: MPK/JK

17th June 1991

Mr M Millionaire
Chairman
Chardock Rangers F.C.
The Allotments
Chardock
Dorset

Dear Mr Millionaire,

Thank you for your interest in our products. You have certainly contacted the right company since, having been paint manufacturers since 1773, we have been involved with many of Britain's sporting institutions since their earliest days.

We do indeed manufacture a full range of specialist products appropriate to your exciting venture, details of which are as follows:-

All purpose "Soccastrip" line paint

Ideal for all straight line work, "Soccastrip" produces a touch line even the blindest linesman could not miss on a dull day in Darlington. Made from naturally occuring ingredients, it will not kill the grass and yet retains a whiteness that would bring Maradona to his knees with anticipation. It comes with its own Matt Green (Wolves and Worcester City) undercoat.

"Soccaflex" Curved Line Paint

Based on a highly flexible resin, Soccaflex produces accurate circles, semi-circles and even the bent bit by the corner flag (or Justin as we call it in the trade).

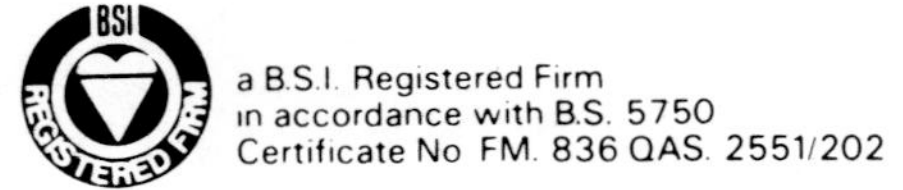

"Refassist" Goal Line Paint

A Specialist product specially formulated for goal lines which reacts to pressure by temporarily turning yellow, thus enabling referees to adjudicate on balls bouncing down from the crossbar. "Refassist" was developed in Manders own laboratories following the controversy surrounding Geoff Hurst's second goal in 1966.

"Soccaspot" High Friction Paint

This brilliant white anti-slip coating produces centre and penalty spots which resist the normal tendency for the ball to blow off the spot at crucial moments.

The Price structure of these products is as follows:-

Soccastrip	- 10 litre can - enough for one full size pitch	£69.50
Soccaflix	- $2\frac{1}{2}$ litre can - enough for one centre circle, two penalty area semi-circles and four Justins	£29.50
Refassist	- 1 litre can - enough for both goal lines	£19.50
Soccaspot	- 500ml pack - enough for a centre spot and two penalty spots.	£14.50

Delivery is free on orders over £100.00.

We would prefer cash with order, but should you wish to open a Credit account this may be possible on production of a glowing bank reference, a personal guarantee signed by yourself, your wife and next of kin, and the written promise of two decent cup final tickets at not too much over the odds.

We would be pleased to be associated with your new venture and look forward to receiving your initial order.

Yours sincerely

~~M P~~ KEEP
MANAGING DIRECTOR
MANDERS DECORATIVE SUPPLIES

CHARDOCK RANGERS FOOTBALL CLUB,THE ALLOTMENTS,CHARDOCK

The Greatest Football Team in the World

(Headed notepaper a bit of a problem at the moment)

Mr Jim French
Atcost Buildings Ltd.,
Spa House,
Tunbridge Wells,
Kent

Dear Jim French,

I have been advised you are the best people for knocking up a one hundred thousand seater stadium.Do you have such a thing in stock?

I need something similar to Wembley,with the exception of the twin towers which would cause obvious problems to light aircraft on crop-spraying duty.

I look forward to your reply in this matter and,by the way,if you deliver in flat packs,I'm sure some of the lads at the Dog and Duck will help to bung it up.

Yours faithfully,

Maurice Millionaire
Club Chairman and DIY Expert
Chardock Rangers Football Club.

Our Ref: Your Ref: Date

18th July 1991

Mr M Millionaire
Chairman
Chardock Rangers FC
The Allotments
Chardock
Dorset

Dear Mr Millionaire

RE: PROPOSED 100,000 SEAT STADIUM

We acknowledge receipt of your reply to our advertisement in this month's issue of Team-Talk, the magazine for non-league football. Your letter has been passed to us by the Post Office as you omitted to put our address on the letter.

We note your requirements for a 100,000 seater stadium and certainly you have come to the right company. Atcost have provided a number of stadia for non-league football clubs, the most recent being for a club in the Vauxhall Conference league. This was for a ground with seating for 10,000 people.

Our structural engineers tell us that we could, in fact, put one stadium on top of another, forming a 10 storey stadium, with the addition of a staircase block at one end. This would provide seating for 100,000 people.

The advantages of this approach are threefold:-

1) All spectators have a superb view of the pitch and, except in the case of low cloud, can enjoy the game in comfort.

2) Bulk buying on our behalf means that the top two stories are FREE!

3) We do not have to prepare new drawings, simply duplicate the old ones.

Continued....

Spa House, 18 Upper Grosvenor Road, Tunbridge Wells, Kent TN1 2EP
Tel: Tunbridge Wells (0892) 26288 Fax: (0892) 515348

Directors: M.W. Stubbs, ACMA (Managing) D.P. O'Loughnane, FCIS (Secretary) L. Moore, C. Eng. MIStructE
Registered Office as above. Registered in London Co. No. 1690866 VAT No. 367 5866 96

We note also your requirement for a Magnolia stadium. This is something of a problem, but one which we can overcome. Magnolia is not a British Standard colour, and is not readily available. However, we have been granted permission from the EEC in Brussels to use this colour, and have already obtained quotations for a special batch of paint. The cost of this is shown separately, in case you wish to consider a standard colour (puce would look very nice).

Our cost for the stadium would be as follows:-

1. Atcost 10 storey stadium to seat 100,000 people	80,000,000
2. Cost of Magnolia paint	25,000,000
	£105,000,000

Our standard conditions of contract would apply, with 50% cash with order and balance as the work proceeds.

We look forward to hearing from you.

Yours sincerely

Jim French

J French
Commercial Manager

CHARDOCK RANGERS FOOTBALL CLUB,THE ALLOTMENTS,CHARDOCK

The Greatest Football Team in the World

(Headed notepaper not in the correct drawer)

Mr Dave Courtney,
3-D Cricket Ltd.,
Cheltenham,
Gloucestershire.

Dear Dave Courtney,

I am Chairman of Chardock Rangers and we are building a huge stadium.I've already sorted the paint out and I'm now looking for some goalposts and nets.I don't think two jumpers slung on the ground is adequate for the European Cup.I mean to say,what would Real Madrid think?

I was wondering if you could knock me a couple up.I would like the netting in yellow,white and brown,our club colours.regarding the posts,I often find unwanted sections of wood floating in rivers.As a matter of fact,that's how we found our centre forward.As the beautiful River Severn is in your vicinity,I suggest you try there.If all else fails,get back to me and I'll send young Alfie Parker up with a trailer full of logs.You will then only have to stick them together and paint them white.

I look forward to a quote.

Yours faithfully,

Maurice Millionaire
Chairman and lumberjack
Chardock Rangers Football Club.

3-D Cricket Limited, The Runnings, Cheltenham, Glos. GL51 9NJ
Tel: (0242) 241819 (3 lines) Fax: 0242-222994 Telex: 43432 DSA G REF 3D

23rd July, 1991.

Maurice Millionaire Esq.,
Chardock Rangers Football Club,
The Allotments,
Chardock.

Dear Mr. Millionaire,

Thank you for your interesting enquiry, I am sure I can help solve your problem. It is an incredible project on behalf of your club, but I do feel you are somewhat presumptuous regarding your place in the European Cup Final. I understand that it is already a foregone conclusion that Cheltenham Town will be playing Real Madrid this season, but with the new stadium and goalposts to match, next season could be the turn of Chardock Rangers!

Now to the goalposts and nets. I would agree that in view of the international games to be played in your stadium, goalposts and nets would need to be of an international standard. Certainly jumpers or even road cones would not suffice at this level, nor dare I hasten to add, chopped down green painted cricket netting poles in which we specialise, but whilst I cannot help from stock, as the proverbial A.A. man says, "I know a man who can". As your club colours are yellow and white, at no extra charge the netting trims and ties can be a psychedelic yellow with white posts and nets. Incidentally as a matter of interest, I understand that a new innovation in netting has recently become available, to make them more durable they are now reversible to make them last longer. Before I offer you a firm quotation perhaps you would confirm that this quality of product, that only a millionaire can afford, would be suitable.

Incidentally, I would be interested to know whether the Alfie Parker you refer to is the Alfie (Nosey) Parker who used to play centre forward for Knotveryathletic in the 50's, before being transferred to Yeovil Town for £12.19s.6d. Perhaps you would enlighten me on this when being next in contact.

I await your reply and thank you for your valued enquiry.

Yours sincerely,

D. J. V. Courtney
Managing Director

Directors: D.J.V. Courtney (Managing), R.A. Teague (Marketing), P.M. Courtney
Resident Consultant: T.W. Graveney O.B.E., Associate: J.H. Edrich M.B.E.

CHARDOCK RANGERS FOOTBALL CLUB,THE ALLOTMENTS,CHARDOCK

The Greatest Football Team in the World

(Headed notepaper unavailable due to rotten quote)

Head Gardener,
The Gardener's Shed,
Wembley Stadium
Middlesex.

Dear Greenfingers,

I understand internationals and cup finals are played on your pitch.Indeed,I myself have been particularly knocked out with your standard of grass,specially at a recent Elton John concert.

I notice you grow your grass in light green and dark green strips,and am wondering as to whether or not I could purchase some used ones from your stadium.

Due to lack of fitness,we intend our playing surface to be only sixty yards.Could we cut the strips in half?

Could you please inform me of the chances ?

Yours faithfully,

Maurice Millionaire
Chairman and keen gardener
Chardock Rangers Football Club.

Mr Maurice Millionaire
Chardock Rangers Football Club
The Allotments
Chardock

Dear Mr Millionaire,

Thank you for your enquiry relating to the Wembley turf.The light and dark green strips you are interested in are achieved by experienced grass cutting and I am afraid they are not for sale.

Creating a football pitch on an allotment obviously has its problems,and all I can suggest to help you is to grow light green and dark green vegetables,say,brussel sprouts and cabbage.I am certain that from a distance this would suffice.

We at Wembley Stadium wish you the very best of luck in the construction of your new stadium and trust the players of Chardock Rangers will serve you proud.

Best wishes,

Head Gardener
Wembley Stadium

Wembley Stadium Limited, Wembley HA9 ODW. Telephone:- Admin:- 081 902 8833, Box Office:- 081 900 1234
Telex: 881173. Fax Nos:- Stadium: 081 900 1055, Conference Centre: 081 903 3234, Direct No

Wembley Stadium Limited (Registered in England No. 223957) Registered Office: The Wembley Stadium HA9 ODW

CHARDOCK RANGERS FOOTBALL CLUB.THE ALLOTMENTS.CHARDOCK.DORSET

The Greatest Football Team in the World

Corporaction.
Corporate Entertainment Specialists
Wokingham
Berkshire

Dear Sirs,

I am building a football stadium for one hundred thousand, in preparation for Chardock Rangers going into Europe.I understand you provide executive boxes.It has been discussed at boardroom level and we have decided to proceed with such boxes because many of our spectators are under five feet tall and will have great difficulty watching our games from the back of the stands.

We require a dozen boxes of different heights,say,six twelve inches high and six fifteen inches high.

Can you confirm you can supply such boxes? If we supplied our own wood would they be cheaper ?

Thanking you in anticipation.I await your reply.

Yours faithfully,

Maurice Millionaire

Maurice Millionaire
Six foot Chairman
Chardock Rangers Football Club.

Maurice Millionaire
Chardock Rangers Football Club,
The Allotments,
Chardock

Dear Mr Millionaire,

Thank you for your letter received today. Executive boxes are not actually what you think they are,but as you seem to be a club destined for European success we will be only too delighted to divert from our usual fixtures of Internationals and Cup Finals by providing your own personal Executive Box requirements for your shorter spectators.

As soon as construction of your new ground is complete will shall be delighted to place some wooden boxes at the back of the stands,upside down of course as we don't want your valuable customers falling in them do we?

Herring boxes seem to be the favoured variety and as your stadium is on the coast we shall have them delivered direct from Hull by trawler,thus saving time and eliminating unsavoury smells in our Mercedes courtesy car.

We look forward to obtaining your confirmation to proceed with the promise of our best attention at all times.

Thank you for your enquiry,

Yours faithfully,

Corporaction
Corporate Entertainment Specialists.

• • •

Kingswood House
12 Shute End, Wokingham, Berks RG11 1BJ
Tel: 0734 894 607 Fax: 0734 894 618

Registered office: 25 The Rise, Edgware, Middlesex HA8 8NS

THE THOUGHTS OF CHAIRMAN MO

It is pretty obvious that things are really starting to move in Chardock.I viewed the bungalow with the large garden which the estate agents suggested but it was sadly unsuitable.It didn't have a television aerial for the half-time reports on the BBC.Those estate agents are trying so hard to fix me up with something.They're out every day searching on my behalf. Well,I assume they are because nobody ever seems to be there to take my telephone call when I phone.

With regards Manders Paints,I have sent off the names and addresses of a few blokes in the East End who can vouch for my good credit.Couldn't sort out a bank reference as I don't have a bank account.I went in the bank once but it was the middle of the night and I got eighteen months.Anyway, Manders circular paint should do the trick when I get hold of some grass.Which reminds me,regarding Wembley Stadium, when I want some advice on how to grow vegetables I'll watch Pebble Mill At One like everyone else.

Atcost Buildings idea of bunging ten,ten thousand seater stadiums on top of each other was brilliant.Sadly,I found the cost a little prohibitive and therefore gave the job to my daughter's boyfriend.He could do with the work and it's on the condition that if he gets my daughter in the family way,he can sling his hook and I'll build the bloody place myself. It looks like the stadium will be a corrugated iron job with a few coats of my favourite magnolia.I've always loved magnolia. I once covered a shifty geezer in it who flogged me a knackered Capri.He looked really summery.He really did.The ground will have a capacity of forty,well under the original estimate, but in these days of recession....beggars can't be choosers.

We have finally managed to come up with our own style of netting.I just hope the ball doesn't get stuck in those lobster pots though because they'll never get the bloody thing out again.So I wrote to 3D Cricket thanking them kindly for their time and trouble,as I finally did Wembley Stadium.

As for Corporaction's executive boxes,I had to draw the line there I'm afraid.How they make millions and millions of pounds flogging old smelly herring boxes and turning them upside down for midgets is beyond me.O.K I'm a millionaire myself,but I did it the hard way.I wasn't born with a silver gemmy in my mouth.I had to flog knackered cars at rip off prices to a bunch of idiots.Yes,I know all that,but at least l took pride in my work.

Oh well,we'd find somewhere to play.The important thing was to add a bit of class,get a decent manager and a hot dog stand.As I said at the beginning,at was pretty obvious that things were really starting to move in Chardock.Perhaps it was that curry.

Chapter Two

The Quest for European Football

Now that the formation of the club,and the stadium in particular, was well in hand,the vital question of club personnel needed some urgent attention.To that end,I stayed behind for a late one at the Dog and Duck,to enable me to discuss and another more immediate matter with Rosie the worthy barmaid.

Who,for instance,Iasked her exhausted,should we choose to be our club manager.We needed someone to guide our carefully hand-picked team of international stars.Should we rely on the home-spun talents of 'The Dorset Doberman' Nudger Dixon,a man steeped in Chardock's football history.A pillar of the local community since his release from Broadmoor.A soccer guru with countless appearances as spongeman in the Dorset Easter Floodlit league.........And he was cheap too.

Rosie,with a twinkle in her eye,suggested someone bigger. For a moment I was gutted until I realised she was talking of the managerial position (probably the only position she'd never tried.)Someone to carry our eternal flame through the cities of Europe,via Dormouth Bus Station.Together we drew up the short list in condensation,long into the night,and most of the next morning.In a haze I remembered most of the ideas and wrote them down.The manager's vacancy,I'd read of a few in the papers I could approach.The referee who could swing a game or two.Well refs are a bunch of tossers anyway,I didn't know a good one from a bad one.

Match reporters,we needed the publicity as we proceeded through Europe.We needed the finest caterers.If not,the loan of someone's barbecue.My plan of a kebab night with frozen mince meat and three cartons of nicked flip-flops,the previous season had been a dismal failure.This time there were to be no mistakes.How could you get the chairman of Barcelona to eat a sandal?.......Come to th.................

No stone was left unturned,and within a month the letters were on their way to the chosen few.Oh yes,and Rosie was expecting a baby.

The short list,drawn up in consultation with the vicar's wife,herself a bit of a scorcher as it happens,but ridiculously out of bounds,made powerful reading.Many had said the woman, though blessed,was a psalm short of a sermon and this was confirmed when I realised she'd written to our local folk heroes, The Tolpuddle Martyrs.A fine local brigade but long since dead. Mrs Vicar stressed they would have made seven worthy directors. I could not argue but for that one minor point.Stupid woman. They were after all,buried in a local churchyard she visited regularly.

One of the remaining candidates ear-marked for football's most rewarding post of Chardock Rangers club manager would surely fit the bill.So it was the manager's position I dealt with first. I sat with Rosie,just the three of us,and after hours of dictation,which I enjoyed thoroughly,letters of invitation were winging their way in optimistic fashion,though temporarily held up by the closure of the Post Office due to a rum and tombola event at the local Fire Station.

CHARDOCK RANGERS FOOTBALL CLUB.THE ALLOTMENTS.CHARDOCK.DORSET

The Greatest Football team in the World

Headed notepaper not on active duty at present

Mr Norman Schwarzkopf,
c/o Chardock Territorial Army,
The Dog and Duck Back Bar
Chardock.

Dear Norman Schwarzkopf,

Well done in Iraq.I thought we won,even if Baghdad Radio claimed a draw.

Are you busy now it's all over ? If not, though I admit your name may not fit on our letter heading and I can't spell it anyway,we would like you to apply for the vacant manager's job at Chardock Rangers.America are apparently staging a World Cup soon,so this could be a chance to pick up some pointers for when you are put in charge of the American team as they struggle early on.

We can offer you a camp in the cowfield and shooting range in our caravan site,but please,no tanks on the pitch as our groundsman kicks up a stink if his finely manicured molehills are disturbed in the penalty areas.

In closing,I should warn you we are unable to call you 'Storming' as our own tea-lady Norma has adopted that nickname herself,and would naturally be upset if anyone should upstage her.Her love bites are frightening.

I look forward to hearing from you.Attention.

Yours faithfully

Maurice Millionaire
Club Chairman,Mentioned in Despatches
Chardock Rangers Football Club.

CHARDOCK RANGERS FOOTBALL CLUB.THE ALLOTMENTS.CHARDOCK.DORSET

The Greatest Football Team in the World

Headed notepaper a very sore point at present

Jack Charlton
The Manager
Republic of Ireland United
Republic of Ireland.

Dear Jack Charlton,

Following your outstanding success in guiding your fellow Irishmen to unprecedented glory in the World Cup Finals in Israel last year,I have decided to offer you the once in a lifetime opportunity to enhance your career and apply for the post of manager of Chardock Rangers.

It may interest you to know we hope to acquire fishing rights at our new spring fed pond/shower room,and lesser anglers than yourelf are already pulling out stickleback/pike hybrids to five and a half pound.That's according to our groundsman in the Dog and Duck the other night.Though I must stress he was pissed.

Please enclose half a dozen stamped addressed envelopes so you eventually receive a reply.

May I just say how I will always cherish the day when you and brother Eddie won the World Cup in 19 whatever it was.We showed those Frenchies we could play...eh...what?

Yours faithfully,

Maurice Millionaire

Maurice Millionaire
Club Chairman with a little Irish Blood
Chardock Rangers Football Club.

FOOTBALL ASSOCIATION OF IRELAND
CUMANN PEILE NA h-ÉIREANN
80 Merrion Square, Dublin 2.
Telephone: 766864/761354/609721 Telex: 91397 Fax: 610931

Dear Mr Millionaire

Thank you for the invitation to be your Manager.Chardock Rangers.The name has a magical ring to it,a new club,new ground,unlimited finance.You could be in the first division in ten years under the new pyramid system.Its a great opportunity,and I gave it a lot of thought.But I must decline your offer, here are some of my reasons.You would never understand my Geordie accent down there Hinny,especially with my Irish twang(How did you know my brother Bobs middle name was Eddie)My mother Cissy would never come,Bingos a pund a card doon there.I have been in the Pub you mention,The Dog and Duck.The Beer was like P___and they did not sell Newcastle Broon.The fishing was a con the Sticklebacks only got up to Two Pounds.You never said anything about Shooting, I need to blast off at something every day.Duck would have done or Dog,even the odd Player who would not do as I told him.No the Irish will do for me, thanks again for the chance to be a household name again.

Yours in Sport

Jack Charlton O B E.

CHARDOCK RANGERS FOOTBALL CLUB.THE ALLOTMENTS.CHARDOCK

The Greatest Football Team in the World

Headed notepaper nearly ready now.

Tommy Docherty,

Chelsea,QPR,QPR,QPR,Aston Villa,Rotherham,Derby County,Hull
Manchester United,Preston?Wolves,Oporto,Sydney Olympic......
and Scotland.

Well,Tom,you've certainly been about haven't you ? It is with much pleasure I am writing to invite you to apply for the manger's job at Chardock.

I understand we are possibly the only club you have not managed in Europe and Australia,so I feel this position will be of great appeal to you.

In your case,I would be happy to offer you a long term contract of say,three or four days,and would respectfully ask that you pledge to fulfil at least half this term before pissing off or forcing me to sack you.

I would not anticipate any loyalty bonuses in your contract and would only write your name in pencil in the match day programme.

If you say you are not interested,I will naturally presume that you are.An early reply from wherever you may be would be greatly appreciated.

Yours faithfully,

Maurice Millionaire

Maurice Millionaire
Chardock Rangers Football Club.

harlesworth Sports Promotions Ltd.

2 Tann Court,
Town Lane,
Charlesworth,
Via Hyde,
Cheshire SK14 6HQ.

Maurice Millionaire,
Chardock Rangers Football Club
The Allotments
Chardock

Dear Maurice,

I hope you don't mind me calling you by your first name,but I feel I already know you.I also feel that Chardock Rangers is my type of club(where have I heard that before?)

You seem to be my kind of chairman(I've heard that somewhere before too).

I was dumbfounded that you only managed to list 14 of the 16 clubs I managed during my career (I think that's what it was)

I would love the job with Chardock Rangers though I apprecia big names will be after the position.I can see it now 'The Doc gets the Job'.I accept all the conditions,after all oney isn't everything,well, not all of the time.There are two things I would like to make clear;
1.Is your Physio married?
2.May I have 4 weeks holiday during each season to allow my annual trip to the Old Bailey,which is not one of my old clubs,though I've spent more time there than I did with Rotherham United.

I will take your club to places you have never been before, including the Old Bailey though you've probably been there a few times yourself Maurice.

Please keep my application private with no leakage to the media.I never speak to them myself.They tell lies you know.Always trust a thief but never a liar.Write soon Maurice as there are loads of clubs chasing me,so don't hesitate or all is lost.
Yours in sport,
Britain's number one manager.Alright,I know you can't get lower than number one.
Best wishes,

Tommy Docherty

CHARDOCK RANGERS FOOTBALL CLUB.THE ALLOTMENTS.CHARDOCK.DORSET

The Greatest Football Team in the World

Headed notepaper delayed in the post.

Mr Lawrie McMenemy,
The Football Association.
16 Lancaster Gate
London.

Dear Lawrie McMenemy,

I am inviting you to apply for the vacant manager's post at Chardock Rangers.I'm led to believe that we are a little ambitious in contacting you but it has been decided by 5 votes to 4,with three spoilt papers,to go for you all the same.

As you are no doubt aware through our extensive advertising campaign in 'Country Life' and 'Bunty',our declared plan is to become the greatest team in the World next season.

Would you please,at your earliest opportunity, confirm your interest in this coveted position with your agreement to undertake night school lessons in the hope of securing an accent a little more condusive to sleepy Dorset.No salary is available, we play on Tuesday afternoons,and we would apprecia acceptance of a reverse charge call should we need to telephone to arrange an interview.

Yours faithfully,

Maurice Millionaire

Maurice Millionaire
Chairman and Territorial Army Member
Chardock Football Club.

THE FOOTBALL ASSOCIATION
LIMITED
Founded 1863

Patron: HER MAJESTY THE QUEEN
President: H.R.H. THE DUKE OF KENT
Chairman: SIR BERT MILLICHIP

Chief Executive:
R. H. G. KELLY FCIS

Phone: 071-402 7151/071-262 4542
Telex: 261110
Facsimile: 071-402 0486

16 LANCASTER GATE, LONDON W2 3LW

Our Ref: *Your Ref:*

Maurice Millionaire
Chardock Rangers Football Club
The Allotments
Chardock
Dorset

Dear Mr Millionaire

Thank you for your kind invitation to manage Chardock Rangers. To say I am flattered is the understatement of the year. I can tell you that Big Ron, El Tel and even Graham Taylor are green with envy.

However, it is with great reluctance that I have to decline the offer. Unfortunately the fact that you require me on Tuesday's rules me out. You see, that is the day I attend classes for elocution which are being run by Kenny Dalglish and Paul Gascoigne who are not doing much in the football line at present.

However, I know you will not have any difficulty in obtaining a big name (if not necessarily a long one) and may I take this opportunity to wish you well and look forward to seeing you in the European Cup Final at the end of next season. So please feel free to continue reversing the charges.

Best wishes.

Yours sincerely

Lawrie McMenemy

THE ROYAL BIRKDALE GOLF CLUB

SOUTHPORT, MERSEYSIDE, PR8 2LX

Here indeed is ample proof of my search for the right man for the right job, for I am reliably informed that within the bunkers and fairways of the above golf club, lurked the most famous and respected sporting folk, sciving off from a hard day's work.

I searched endlessly for the former manager of Liverpool, Kenny Dalglish, but nowhere could I see the famous red shirt. A voice echoed in the distance bearing a similiarity to that of Mr Dalglaish, but upon further inspection it turned out to be a water vole trying to pull a mate for the summer.

For a few days I sat by the sixteenth but to no avail, other than the fact that I heard the complete repertoire of Jimmy Tarbuck. I returned down the motorway thinking that the job could well go to Nudger Dixon after all, though it was against my wishes, the thieving bastard.

I wrote to Nudger that evening, knowing his reply would be in crayon as sharp pointed instruments were not allowed where Nudger resided.

Maurice Millionaire
Below par.

CHARDOCK RANGERS FOOTBALL CLUB.THE ALLOTMENTS.CHARDOCK.DORSET

The Greatest Football Team in the World

Headed notepaper not wasted on idiots.

Nudger Dixon.
The Floor of the Dog and Duck.
Chardock.

Dear Nudger,

Due to your local knowledge,availability and stories I know you don't want me to spread,I'm inviting you to apply for the manager's job.

If hell freezes over and you should be successful,I trust you will treat the position with a little more professionalism than at the Dog the other night.I also stress the acceptance of this post will also signal the end of your drinking fifteen pints of Scrumpy and farting 'You'll Never Walk Alone'to the accompaniment of Lily Fanshawe's tambourine.

Lets face it Nudger old son,you haven't got a dog's chance,but drop me a line anyway.

Your old mate.

Maurice Millionaire

Dear Maurice

—

Thanks for inviting me to apply for manager of Charnock F.C. I have 2 GCEs in metalwork and shopping.

and I now I now nothing about any sport

I would like £3 per week and a free drink vougher at the dog and Duck. As for the farting, I shall try to contain myself by the way my new rendition is Bohemian Rhapsody though an unfortunate I accident occured during Galileo. I presume Jack Charlton or Tommy doc will get the Job But if not I will take it on if you tell me what to do

yours

Nudger Dixon

Ps Please excuse hand writing, I'm StupiD

After much thought and discussion,in a horizontal position, with Rosie,we were,to say the least,a little disappointed. Jack Charlton had a side that would never play in the English First Division,Lawrie Guardsman was tied up,leaving Tommy Docherty,football legend.It did occur to us what may happen two weeks after we had given him the job,we'd have to go through it all again.So we decided against the Doc and I penned a note and pinned it on the dart board at the Dog and Duck.

'Nudger,

You start on Monday,

The Chairman.

Administration continued throughout forthcoming months. Chardock Rangers was getting bigger by the day......as was Rosie

Chapter Three

Helping Hands

CHARDOCK RANGERS REPORT

I never knew a football club needed so many people behind the scenes,did you ? For instance,did you know every game needed a referee and two linesmen?My God,the last time I saw men waving flags was on the platform at Axminster Station.

The physiotherapist was needed to heal injuries and a doctor was required to sort out nasty things picked up in the discos at away match trips.Champion jockey,a brave man,once supplied with a good tip.he told me to move or his horse would break my foot.Another idea he gave me was to contact Mr Terry Mott at Ipswich Hospital in Suffolk. This I did.

I then scribbled time-consuming letters to apply for immediate entry into the Football League Second Division. It was blatantly obvious to me such promotion went without saying with a manger like Nudger Dixon,and a footballer like David Gower.Yes,it went without saying,and many wrote to never said.

I wrote to the Allied Irish Bank in the Channel Islands,hoping their knowledge of football club sponsorship was as classy as their geography skills.Allied Irish Bank in Jersey ? Iask you.The club needed yellow and white striped shirts and brown shorts,a colourful tradition started a hundred years ago by the Chardock Brownies.Match commentators and local radio coverage.Lottery ticket salesmen.Deary me,the list would have been well over a mile long had I not set fire to it.

The programmes,I forgot the programmes.Who would design them? Who would take on a print run that varied between one hundred thousand and forty seven ?

Half-time entertainment was another point to consider and a subject in which I was well versed since booking the rock band for my grandmother's wedding (she didn't want to get married,she had to).My idea of a couple of good beefy strippers in yellow and white hooped stockings was sadly met with great disapproval and rejected out of hand by the headmaster of Chardock Primary School.He insisted he hadn't worn such things for years.

CHARDOCK RANGERS FOOTBALL CLUB.THE ALLOTMENTS.CHARDOCK

The Greatest Football Team in the World

Headed notepaper far too expensive

Mr Gordon Taylor,
Professional Footballers Association.
Bishopsgate
Manchester.

Dear Gordon Taylor,

Whenever a football topic is discussed,your name seems to pop up on teletext as some sort of spokesman for everyone.So although I am not too certain exactly what it is you do,you seem to be important enough to help my new club Chardock Rangers on a small matter of procedure.How do we cut all the pissing about and go straight into the Second Division ? Could you possibly send us the necessary form of application and,indeed,perhaps you'll fill it in for me and I'll just sign the bottom when I find the time.

I'm sure a word from you in the right lugholes will cut out any silly paperwork which only clutters up my desk and confuses my filofax.

So whatever it is you do,I look forward to receiving the completed form.

Yours faithfully,

Maurice Millionaire
Chairman
Chardock Rangers Football Club.

Professional Footballers Association
2 Oxford Court, Bishopsgate, Manchester M2 3WQ
Telephone: 061-236 0575 Fax: 061-228 7229 Telex: 265871 MONREF G (Quote Ref: CXX004)

Chief Executive: Gordon Taylor M.A., B.Sc. (Econ.)

17th September, 1991

Mr. Maurice Millionaire,
Chardock Rangers F.C.,
The Allotments,
Chardock.

Dear Maurice,

I am so pleased that you study the teletext - such a wonderfully brief and superficial way of absorbing the significance of the many deep and varied nuances of the labyrinth world of football. I like that in a chairman, it shows commitment.

I am at a loss to understand why your ambition is only to join the Second Division of the Football League. I would have thought a man of your obvious taste, tact and experience would have felt happiest in the boardrooms of our Premier Clubs.

The form that would enable you to bribe your way into the Second Division has, fortunately, not yet been devised. Sadly, it may be just a matter of time before it is. However, the people who may be able to help you are the Football Association. They are the "Governing Body" you should contact. To them your vast fortune could be seen as a suitable qualification for your entry into the top level of our national game. You appear to speak the same language as they do as according to the media they and the Super League clubs are also motivated by 'greed & avarice'.

You will feel much more satisfied if you obtained promotion on merit but should you succeed in your totally unworthy endeavour which in the present climate is not impossible please do not contact me again. I will have thrown in the towel and left the country, having taken the easier option of earning my living crocodile wrestling in deepest Australia.

Yours sincerely,

Gordon Taylor

GORDON TAYLOR
Chief Executive.

P.S. Just a small point but the name and address of your club concern me - they definitely don't have the right smell of success about them. A man in your position, with his finger on the pulse, his nose on the grindstone, his feet firmly on the ground, his shoulder on the wheel and his bottom on the executive loo really should have realised everything is in a name!!

Gordon Taylor surprised me with his knowledge.How I wished he was the new Chardock Member of Parliament instead of that silly old fart who'd been done for field crawling.

I took up Gordon's point regarding the Football Aristocrats,the bosses of the game that was beginning to piss me off.I enquired as to whether or not there was a special form for sneaking into the Premier League,as suggested,by Gordon,thus accepting his point that there seemed little chance of reaching Europe via the Second Division.I therefore failed to work out how Dover,the nearest town to the Europeans weren't in any of the top divisions.I don't know any more.I'm confused.

I wrote to the governing bodies complaining on behalf of Dover,and I think the two worded reply opposite sorted everything out in my mind.

I pondered upon who actually had written those two superb words.It could have been any one of a thousand famous footballers. Stanley Matthews,Nat Lofthouse,Johnny Haynes,Rachel Hey Ho Silver Lining.Each day I imagined a different author until I settled for Samantha Fox and Kim Bassinger,though in a similar way I must say I also had great respect for Gordon Banks.

TELEPHONE
ST. ANNES 729421
(STD 0253)

TELEGRAMS:
"LEAGUE" ST. ANNES

TELEX:
67675

THE FOOTBALL LEAGUE LIMITED

REG. NO. 80612
ENGLAND

REGISTERED OFFICE
LYTHAM ST ANNES
LANCS.
FY8 1JG.

SECRETARY:
R. H. G. KELLY, F.C.I.S.

NO COMMENT!

All Correspondence to be addressed to THE SECRETARY

CHARDOCK RANGERS FOOTBALL CLUB.THE ALLOTMENTS.CHARDOCK

The Greatest Football Team in the World

Mr Jack Taylor,
World Cup Referee.
Ref's Headquarters
London.

Dear Jack Taylor,

As the above club wends its way to football immortality,it occurs to me it might be useful to have the same referee for every game.Naturally,this man would have to be someone we can trust,and whilst you don't fit the category, your name has been mentioned.

I gather you once gave a penalty during the team presentations before the World Cup Final in 1970 something. I feel that similar aberrations could greatly enhance our chances of winning every week.We don't expect favouritism,but your position as club referee will be reviewed on a match to match basis....as will your lift home.

Please let me know if you are still refereeing Cup Finals on a regular basis and if there is one you are doing in the next few weeks that I can watch to assess your suitability and swear at you.

Yours faithfully,

Maurice Millionaire
Chairman and Fair Man
Chardock Rangers Football Club

8 October 1991

Mr Maurice Millionaire
Chardock Rangers FC
The Allotments,
Chardock

Dear Maurice

Thank you for your undated letter sent to the wrong address - it was much appreciated and as someone who did not fit into the category of being not known or trusted, it also made an old style past referee feel wanted.

You are reasonably correct in your assumption that I did referee a World Cup Final, but it was in 1974 and not in 1970 as stated by you, which again enhances your knowledge of soccer thereby convincing me that you will go a long way as a football club chairman - and I really do hope, the further the better.

With regard to refereeing Chardock Rangers Football Club, I can only suggest you contact your County Football Association, should you know what that is. If not I am sure Lancaster Gate would fill you in with further details on the game we all love.

.../2

In answer to your final paragraph, I no longer referee so it will be impossible for you to assess me. However, if I can help to improve your ground at The Allotments, Chardock or suggest ways in which to promote your club, particularly the areas in which you would wish to invest, I do work for the Football League Commercial Division, which is so good at investing other people's money for the benefit of all involved with the greatest game in the world.

If all else fails, I would not like you to think I was being unco-operative and I could be available to officiate for your club on a Monday or Thursday afternoon, when I am sure we could negotiate a fee.

Yours faithfully

JACK TAYLOR, OBE, JP

ToMaurice Millionaire
From,Sir Geoffrey Boycott

Dear Mr Millionaire,

Following our telephone conversation this morning,may I thank you for reversing the charges and inviting me to adjudicate your man of the match awards for the coming football season.

Unfortunately I have to decline your most generous offer as I will be commentating on Test Matches abroad during this period.

I am sorry to be of no help on this particular occasion but may I take this opportunity of wishing your club every success in Europe

Yours sincerely,

Sir Geoffrey Boycott.

CHARDOCK RANGERS FOOTBALL CLUB.THE ALLOTMENTS.CHARDOCK

The Greatest Football Team in the World

Headed notepaper out of print.

Mr Tony Williams
Football Directories
The Paper Shop
Chardock

Dear Tony Williams,

Not wishing to beat about the bush,we now have six players and we're on course for the European Cup Final. It looks likely I'll be signing David Gower in the next few days (whatever position he plays).

I write to you as a knowledgeable football journalist because I'd like immediate entry into the Second Division,thus skipping the usual red tape relating to non-league membership.Do you know anyone who can fiddle this ? Will they take readies ?

When I win the cup I will be only too pleased to speak with you.Ring next Autumn when I have secured either a secretary or an answerphone.

Yours faithfully,

Maurice Millionaire.
Professional Chairman
Chardock Rangers Football Club.

Football Directories

Publisher: Tony Williams

The F.A. Non League Club Directory
The Non League Football Grounds of Great Britain
The Non League Footballers' Who's Who

Maurice Millionaire Esq.,
Chardock Rangers F.C.
(T.G.F.T. in T.W.),
The Allotments,
Chardock,
Dorset

Dear Mr Millionaire

Thank you for your letter concerning Chardock Rangers. I circulated your aims and ambitions to a number of Football League Secretaries and The F.A. and have had a number of encouraging replies:

1. The Football Association: Maurice who?
2. The Football League: I think I remember him at New Brighton Football Club.
3. The G.M.V.C.: Probably a friend of that nice Mr Arif of Fisher Athletic.
4. The Diadora League: If he could sponsor 'The Substitute of the Month' Award his team could probably take the place of Vauxhall Motors F.C.
5. The Beazer Homes League: Our ground inspectors will be at The Allotment next Monday.
6. The H.F.S. Loans League: Didn't his team play as West Allotment Celtic in The Northern Alliance?

If you would like to take advantage of any of these openings please let The Football Association know. However, may I suggest for quicker recognition, send in a match card with full details as expected by The Barclays League for your comprehensive victory over Aldershot on the first Saturday of the season. Follow this with equally comprehensive reports of victories over each League club having a free Saturday and perhaps the name of 'Leytonstone-Ilford-Walthamstow Avenue' will be treated with sympathy by old F.A. and League officials. This subtle name change might just tip the balance in your favour if F.A. Councillors get a vote.

You will find, if regularly successful against Fourth Division clubs on their free day, the match report cards should be impressive enough to win you the new 'Leyland Daffodil Consistency European' Award and a place in the U.E.F.A. Cup in 1992-93.

May I wish you every success and I can assure you that your progress will be monitored in future issues of Team Talk.

Yours sincerely

Tony Williams

CHARDOCK RANGERS FOTTBALL CLUB.THE ALLOTMENTS.CHARDOCK.DORSET

The Greatest Football Team in the World

Headed notepaper delayed due to spelling missttakes

Mike Payne
Artist.
The Art Shop
Chardock

Dear Mike Payne,

Due to unfortunate bouts of food poisoning from a dubious chinky the other night,my wife is ill.We received a get well card which was drawn by yourself.

Any chance of knocking up a programme ? Art isn't my strong point,the only other picture I've seen was Constable's 'Haywain' and some little sod had coloured THAT in. Perhaps you could combine that with one of your teddy bears, leaving enough space to put the teams.

I look forward to hearing from you and,as my previous job was selling second hand cars,may I suggest a card along the lines of 'Sorry to hear you've had your legs broken John.' What do you think ?

Yours faithfully,

Maurice Millionaire
Chairman and art lover
Chardock Rangers Football Club.

Mike Payne..
C.C.G.B.
F.E.C.O.
Angmering, West Sussex.

Our Ref:

Your Ref:

Date:

18 July 1991

CHARDOCK RANGERS FOOTBALL CLUB
The Allotments
Chardock

Dear Mr Millionaire,

Thank you for yor letter and for the offer of a commission for the programme of Chardock Rangers.

I'm flattered that you liked my artwork on the card to the extent that you have asked me to contribute. Unfortunately, as luck would have it, just prior to receiving your letter I have accepted a commission for designing Greeting Cards which should take me ~~15~~ 20 years - otherwise I would gladly have contributed.

Your idea of having the haywain and teddy bears is certainly a little ~~odd~~ different for a football programme and might well appeal to some artist/cartoonist. (Perhaps Rolf Harris might be available).

May I wish you every success with 'The Rangers',

Yours sincerely,

Mike Payne..

Mike Payne

P.S. Thank you for the Card idea but we did that design three years ago worldwide and sold two.

CHARDOCK RANGERS FOOTBALL CLUB.THE ALOTMENTS.CHARDOCK

The Greatest Football Team in the World

Headed notepaper under tender at present

Paper Plane Publishing
c/o The Print Works
c/o The Dog and Duck
Chardock

Dear Phil Walder,

As publishers of football programmes on behalf of large European clubs like ourselves,I'd like you to print a few for us.As you print for Queens Park Rangers,West Bromwich Albion and Wolverhampton Wanderers,you obviously have the experience to undertake our games which take place on Tuesdays when there isn't a game of skittles on.

We are signing International stars and can already confirm Ernie Dredge will be our number 4,if this helps.Further selection will take place ten minutes before kick off.Are you able to print between one hundred thousand and forty seven programmes in ten minutes and deliver them to Chardock in time for kick off ?

If not,an old West Bromwich Albion one will do,together with a huge bucket of Tippex.

If that seems unlikely I will consider you totally uncooperative and return to my John Bull Printing Outfit.

Yours faithfully,

Maurice Millionaire
Fiver printing a speciality
Chardock Rangers Football Club.

PAPER PLANE PUBLISHING LTD

FORGE HOUSE, FORGE LANE, CRADLEY HEATH, WARLEY, WEST MIDLANDS B64 5AL Tel (0384) 410531 Fax (0384) 410113

Reg. No. 2410418 Vat. No. 488 2582 00

Dear Mr Milllionaire

I can honestly say that, in spite of the fact that we have been producing football programmes for a number of years, and currently produce the Wolves, West Brom and Queen's Park Rangers programmes, and have even produced an England international programme for Wembley, to be associated with Chardock Rangers would be a particular honour for us.

The reputation of your team has reached the West Midlands and I was only reading recently, in the Cradley and Netherton Sprout Growers Gazette, about the quality of the vegetables at 'The Allotments', and I hear the coaching staff aren't bad as well.

As I'm sure you know all printers are simply waiting for their customers to call and so, when you provide the information for your match programme on an impossibly short deadline, you will naturally expect delivery before kick off. Our printers, Cradley Print Ltd, have a team of expert printers standing around doing nothing just waiting for your call, so printing 100,000 programmes in nine minutes shouldn't be too much of a problem.

However, the difficulty could well be delivery. What I'd like to suggest is that we hire a helicopter for Tuesday afternoons. This would not only mean rapid delivery, but great publicity, as a parachutist, trailing smoke in team colours of course, could then leap out above the stadium, with the programmes, and make a spectacular entrance.

Additionally, if the pitch was waterlogged, as I understand from time to time is a bit of a problem at 'The Allotments', then the 'copter could hover low over the pitch assisting in the drying operation.

With regard to the supply of old programmes for you to amend, this might be possible, but we would need to know the opposition so that we can search through our extensive library of back issues currently stored in a shoe box under my desk, and find the corresponding fixture from one of our clubs (though I can't quite recall when any of them last played Atletico Upper Piddle).

Finally, I should point out that we have the very latest in new technology which will assist in the rapid production of the programme by using fax machines and modems to transfer page proofs to the Chardock sub Post Office. Am I right in assuming that your left back Bert Tapplethwaite is still the post man? (I well remember that vicious deflection off Bert that knocked you out of the Dorset Pigeon Fanciers Consolation Cup – 'In Off The Postie' were the headlines afterwards as I recall). If so, it would be ideal training for him to rush to your plush offices, next to the milking parlour, with our latest transmission.

I would be pleased to offer a new set of bicycle clips and a puncture repair kit as an incentive to obtain this prestigious contract.

I certainly hope the attached quote will be of interest and I look forward to hearing from you soon.

Yours sincerely

Phil Walder
Paper Plane Publishing Ltd

Attached Quote

Football...causeth fighting, brawling, contention, quarrel picking, murder, homicide and great effusion of blood, as daily experience teacheth. Philip Stubbes (c 1580) Anatomy of Abuses.

CHARDOCK RANGERS FOOTBALL CLUB.THE ALLOTMENTS.CHARDOCK DORSET

The Greatest Football Team in the World

Headed notepaper printer taken ill yesterday

Mr T.J.Mott MB BS FRCS FRCR
Department of Clinical Oncology
Ipswich Hospital
Suffolk.

Dear Mr Mott,

Bloody hell,you've got more letters behind your name than the bloke who invented Scrabble.It was either Bob Champion or Aldaniti who suggested I write offering the post of club surgeon. Interested ?

Your role will be to perform operations at half-time whether necessary or not and give the needed jabs when we visit far flung areas of the globe in search of world domination.

We have no money so you'll have to supply your own bandages and stretchers,though the Dog and Duck are quite prepared to offer neat alcohol to friends of the injured.

Payment will be a time share caravan in beautiful Chardock,Christmas Eve and Boxing Day,shared with Miriam Stoppard. Thank you for your attention.Do you do iffy doctor's certificates ?

Yours faithfully,

[signature] (DR)

Chairman
Chardock Rangers Football Club.

SP5069

DEPARTMENT OF CLINICAL ONCOLOGY

T. J. MOTT F.R.C.S., F.R.C.R.
C. R. WILTSHIRE M.R.C.P., F.R.C.R.

THE IPSWICH HOSPITAL
ANGLESEA ROAD WING
IPSWICH IP1 3PY
Telephone No. 212477 Ext. 258/9

TJM/HJC

21st August 1991.

Mr. M. Millionaire
Chardock Rangers Football Club
The Allotments
Chardock.

Dear Mr. Millionaire,

Re: Club Surgeon for Chardock Rangers.

It was kind of Bob Champion to mention my name. We shared several happy evenings at concerts for our respective charities listening to the up-and-coming Richard Digance. Thank you for the wonderful offer. Chardock could become the pinnacle of my medical career.

I first watched football as a small boy, just after the war, at Charlton. "The Valley" would be packed to watch Sam Bartram (best uncapped goalkeeper in England) take a goal kick and hitch up his shorts in mid run. During every game he would dribble the ball to the half-way line to the intense enjoyment of the crowd. When you are on the F.A.Council, I hope you will insist that every goalkeeper should do a "half-way dribble" twice each half or miss the next match.

Despite sending back to play one of our team with a broken leg last season, I am happy to report that I have been re-appointed as doctor to the Ipswich Rugby Club. In competitive rugby a doctor must authenticate a substitution and take off an injured player. I deny absolutely the accusation that I removed the opposition's best player because of 'bandy legs' last year.

Two years ago I had the honour to act as stand-in for the club doctor at Ipswich Town F.C. I was very apprehensive. There was a telephone under my seat. "If it rings it's serious", I was told. It rang. My heart froze. I answered it. "Hello love, it's Aston Villa, what's the half time score?" said a cheerful Brummy voice. It was then that I met your 'scout' looking for a cheap doctor.

Sadly, my contract with the N.H.S. keeps me at Ipswich for most of the year and I must decline your kind offer. I suggest you try Dr. Sidney Underlay of the local Axminster Carpet Hospital (he was once a good sweeper), and I hope he won't give you the 'brush off'.

With regrets and best wishes,
Yours sincerely,

Terry Mott.

T. J. MOTT.

CHARDOCK RANGERS FOOTBALL CLUB.THE ALLOTMENTS.CHARDOCK

The Greatest Football Team in the World

Headed notepaper injured.

Bryan Robson
Manchester United FC
Old Trafford
Manchester

Dear Bryan Robson,

Hopefully this letter finds you in good health, although I realise the chances are slim.Good news,I have decided to offer you the job of physio.As you've had most knocks and scrapes attributed to the rigours of football I can't believe there isn't an injury you don't know how to mend.

We promise to keep Tommy Docherty away from you and you will need to be in attendance Tuesday afternoons.

Come down to Dorset and meet the lads(we'll keep our fingers crossed you manage the journey unscathed.) I've also told our local Hospital Radio you'll be available for interviews when admitted to casualty.

I await your reply Robbo.

Yours faithfully,

Maurice Millionaire
Chairman and First Aid expert
Chardock Rangers Football Club.

Bryan Robson OBE

TESTIMONIAL
YEAR 1990/91

Dear Mr Millionaire,

Thank you very much for the invitation to be your club physio. At the time of writing this letter I was seriously considering your kind offer, but unfortunately I have just broken my finger while writing.

Appologies for keeping you waiting for this paragraph but my finger has just healed.

You are quite right that there are not too many injuries I have not had, but unfortunately I'm not qualified in dealing with blisters and cutting nails which are ~~more~~ common injuries with footballers. Therefore I will have to decline your kind offer as physio.

Another reason I could not possibly take the job, Tuesday's are my horse racing day's, which I cannot give up even for Chardock Rangers.

Yours sincerely,
Bryan Robson.

CHARDOCK RANGERS FOOTBALL CLUB.THE ALLOTMENTS.CHARDOCK

The Greatest Football Team in the World

Headed notepaper not tax deductable

Mr Sean O'Sullivan
Allied Irish Bank
Jersey
Channel Islands.

Dear Sean O'Sullivan,

Your address disturbs me.I can't recall the Irish invasion of the Channel Islands.It must be bad enough living near those Frenchies,let alone friendly nations having a pop too.

I am seeking a bank loan to buy eleven international footballers and some hardboard to build those advertising signs round the ground.

If I do not hear from you in the next week, I shall assume the Channel Islands have been recaptured and you have been sent back to Ireland with your tails between your legs.

Yours faithfully,

Maurice Millionaire
Chardock Rangers Football Club

AIB Bank (CI) Limited

AIB House
PO Box 468
Grenville Street
St Helier
Jersey
JE4 8WT
Channel Islands

Telephone
General enquiries
(0534) 36633
Deposit enquiries
(0534) 32220
Facsimile
(0534) 31245
Telex
4192394

Our Ref: SOS/ml

21st August, 1991

Mr. M. Millionaire,
Chairman,
Chardock Rangers Football Club,
The Allotments,
CHARDOCK

Dear Mr. Millionaire,

Thank you for your recent letter which, I must say, surprised me on two counts. Firstly, it surprised me that you had not learned earlier of our invasion of the Channel Islands and, secondly, that this is the last Bank to which you have chosen to put your innovative and intriguing proposal. I would have thought that a man like you, who is obviously outstanding in his own field (or pitch), would have known that this Bank is renowned for its fulsome support of all areas of human endeavour, both intellectual and sporting. Indeed, CITIUS ALTUS FORTIS could be our motto, but it isn't.

I have studied your proposal with interest and, it has to be said, a great deal of enthusiasm. I am impressed with the obvious balance you have managed to strike between ambition and financial prudence, a point very much in your favour, though I really think that, to have strengthened your case, you should have asked for an extra £90 or so to facilitate the purchase of a world-class substitute. The exciting prospect of Chardock Rangers competing in the European and World Cups is also viewed most favourably, particularly against the background of complimentary tickets, free bars and post-match dinners which would undoubtedly accrue to the successful team's primary bankers.

Notwithstanding the foregoing, however, it is with regret that I must advise that your proposal has been declined. You see, being an Irish Bank, we have always been 'green' and the prospect of committing Bank funds to a project involving the substantial use of non-recycled products such as hardboard and oil-based paint is one which my Board would not countenance. Perhaps you could study alternative means of providing advertising hoardings, for example compressed meusli boards, organically grown flower arrangements, etc. However, even if you could overcome that problem, there remains the question of collateral value. In a forced sale situation, for instance, what would be the scrap value of a world-class player? In this regard, perhaps you should refer to Mr. Venebales of Tottenham Hotspur Plc.

I am sorry that I could not be more favourable in my response, but I would like to wish you and Chardock Rangers all success in the future.

Yours sincerely,

S O'Sullivan

S. O'Sullivan,
Managing Director

Directors; Jurat P.F. Misson (Chairman), W.J. Morvan, P.R. Douglas, T.P. Mulcahy, J.W. O'Sullivan

AIB Bank (CI) Limited Member of AIB Group Incorporated in Jersey, Channel Islands.

CHARDOCK RANGERS FOOTBALL CLUB.THE ALLOTMENTS.CHARDOCK

The Greatest Football team in the World

Headed notepaper delayed

The Station Master
Axminster Station
Devon

Dear Station Master,

I have followed the lives of station staff through Thomas the Tank Engine videos.It occurs to me that a few years ago you probably had a couple of chaps waving green and red flags at the trains.

Do you know there whereabouts ? I need two linesmen for a European Cup match and if they know nothing about offside and speak no languages they will be ideal.

Any chance of getting them out of retirement?

I hope you can help.Is there any way you can sell Chardock Rangers scarves in your buffet cars ?

Yours faithfully,

Maurice Millionaire
Chardock Rangers Football Club.

To Mr. M. Millionaire,
Chardock Rangers F.C.,
The Allotments,
CHARDOCK.

From Station Master,
British Rail (Southern),
Station Yard,
AXMINSTER,
Devon.
EX13 5PF.

Tel Axminster (0297) 32168

y/r

Ref SM.460

Date

Date 16th August 1991.

Dear Mr. Millionaire,

CHARDOCK RANGERS FOOTBALL CLUB.

Thank you for your recent letter concerning the possibility of our providing linesmen for your forthcoming European Campaign.

The two men in question Robert Parker, of 13 Railway Cuttings, Combpyne Rousdon and Peter Reid, who now lives in a large suitcase in the former left luggage office at Seaton Junction, must inevitably know more about football than they did about railways, although this is not saying much. They certainly know nothing about offside in football, even after careers spanning 49 and 50 years respectively they had very little idea what it meant on the railway.

However, I am concerned about their ability to decide whether or not a player is speaking English. During their time on the Railway it was patently obvious that they had little understanding of the English Language, how else could you explain their consistent failure to follow simple everyday instructions such as, "Sweep the platform" or, "A Superawaybreaklowpricedsaver may be used for travel on any train except, the 0630 to Llanfairpwllgwyngyllgogerychwyrndrobwllllantysiliogogogoch (change at Llandudno Junction), the 0735 to Achnashellach, the 0745 to Luxulyan, the 0800 to Pantyffynnon and various other services too numerous to mention, it is valid for travel on any day, except Fridays, Saturdays in July and August, certain other services during peak holiday periods, when there is an r in the month or if the Booking Clerk has got out of bed on the wrong side".

Continued ....

With reference to the sale of scarves in buffet cars previous experience indicates that this may not be too successful. During our last attempt at such diversification the Norwich City scarves were taken away by the carriage cleaners, who thought they were dusters, some little old ladies picked up anything red, which they then waved out of the window to stop the driver on a farm crossing close to where they lived and the Crossing Keeper at Axe Gates, who used to keep one gate open and one closed because he was half expecting a train, helped himself to those from the Republic of Ireland, on the grounds that they enabled him to keep things moving.

Assuring you of our best attention at all times, unless you wish to travel by train in which case it is cancelled due to, short staffages, long staffages, poor visibility in the Solent, Aardvarks on the line at Longleat, or plain lack of interest.

Yours sincerely,

A. Baldrick,
Station Master.

CHARDOCK RANGERS FOOTBALL CLUB.THE ALLOTMENTS.CHARDOCK

The Greatest Football Team in the World

Headed notepaper still a pain in the bum.

Ron Atkinson
Aston Villa
Villa Park
Birmingham

Dear Ron Atkinson,

Hopefully this letter will finally reach you as I have recently written to numerous clubs only to be told you had moved on.

We are already indebted to you for not wasting our time in applying for our vacant manager's position,but,we request,on a weekly basis,loan of you r first team Aston Villa shirts and shorts.I hate claret and blue,Ron,can you play future games in yellow and white striped shirts and brown shorts ?
In the unlikely event that the kit needs laundering after your own matches,we would undertake this and forward you the bill.
For all this help in our European campaign,we'll fit in a friendly for you against our reserve side next year,if it doesn't clash with skittles.

Please let me know if you change clubs between receiving this letter and replying,and congratulations on your stunning performance in Black Adder.

Yours faithfully

Big Mo
Chardock Rangers Football Club

Aston Villa

ASTON VILLA FOOTBALL CLUB PLC
Registered Office:
Villa Park, Birmingham B6 6HE
Club Offices: 021-327 2299
Ticket Office: 021-327 5353
Credit Card Sales: 021-327 7373
Fax: 021-322 2107. Telex: 334695 VILLA

RA/SFB

16 September 1991

Mr M Millionaire
Chairman
Chardock Rangers Football Club
The Allotments
Chardock
Dorset

Dear Maurice

Many thanks for your recent letter, from which I was somewhat aggrieved to realise that I had missed the opportunity of applying for your vacant managerial post.

It has been my life-long ambition to manage a team which would also enable me to endulge in my love of gardening and I am sad that the opportunity to show what I can do at "The Allotments" has passed me by.

Nevertheless, as befits a man who is known world-wide as Big Ron, I am a stout-hearted fellow and I am only too pleased to confirm that you can borrow our strip on a weekly basis, free of charge. Moreover, I can see no problem in accommodating your desired change to yellow and white striped shirts and brown shorts. In fact, after the rollocking I gave the team last week, most of them are already wearing the shorts. By the way, don't worry about laundering it, because we gave up that lark some time ago. Nobody chases our lads all over the pitch any more, especially when the wind is going straight for the Holte End.

With regard to the possibility of a friendly match, before we can give serious consideration to this request, perhaps you can confirm whether your reserve side is your first choice second team players or your second choice first team players.

Fixing a date for such a match may, however,present us with some problems, because we suffer exactly the same type of demands for players as you experience. When I tell you that only last week we had three players with the England darts team, two with the North Birmingham over 16 tug-of-war team and three in the All England indoor hang-gliding finals, you will see what I mean. On top of all this, to add insult to injury, Graham Taylor had the nerve to call one of them up for the England squad.

Finally, may I say how much I appreciate your kind comments on my performance in Blackadder. It was a lovely little cameo role and the frock and the tights really helped me to get into the part.

Yours sincerely,

RON ATKINSON
MANAGER

Chardock Rangers Football Club, The Allotments,

Chardock, Dorset

The Greatest Football Team In The World

Mr. David Pleat,
England Footballer and Luton Town Manager.
Italy and England.

Dear David Pleat,

I am a little baffled as to how you can manage Luton as well as play in Italy, but presumably flights are easy these days from Luton Airport.

I am inviting you to Chardock Rangers, not to do team talks as we hope to win a few matches, but to lead the community singing. Being versed in Italian and Lutonese you will be very useful in leading the bilingual renditions of Chardock, Chardock, our club song which recently was only marginally rejected by Madonna and Luciano Pavarotti.

Would you please consider this unusual position and a prompt reply would be welcome, and should you come to Chardock, don't go on about scoring that goal on the volley for England in the World Cup as we're all sick to death of seeing it.

Yours faithfully,

Maurice Millionaire
Chardock Rangers Football Club

LUTON TOWN FOOTBALL AND ATHLETIC CO LIMITED

Kenilworth Road Stadium, 1 Maple Road, Luton, Beds. LU4 8AW
Tel: 0582 411622 Telex: 825115 (Ansa back: Bureau G)
Fax: 0582 405070

CHAMPIONS – DIVISION 3(S) 1936/37
FINALISTS – FA CUP 1958/59
CHAMPIONS – DIVISION 4 1967/68
CHAMPIONS – DIVISION 2 1981/82
FINALISTS – SIMOD CUP 1987/88
WINNERS – LITTLEWOODS CUP 1987/88
FINALISTS – LITTLEWOODS CUP 1988/89

Registered Office: 1 Maple Road, Luton, Beds. LU4 8AW Registered No. 53130

Dear Mr Millionaire,

I feel quite humbled by your interest but not the least bit surprised. The tabloids have been full of your successful business projects, your holiday homes empire, your lovely team of secretaries and of course your beloved Chardock Rangers.

My wife remarked what a charming man you are and what a long way you have come since you phoned me five years ago regarding the vacancy at Chipping Sudbury.

However I think we need to clarify my position. I am under contract and AM THE MAN that has made millions for Luton, Tottenham and Leicester. Not to be confused with Pratt, Platt or Plonker. David Platt now volleying for fun in the sun, has never suffered managerial headaches.

As you are aware I have dabbled and coped with two famous politicians in my career. David Evans M.P. and Irving Scholar P.M. so I am fully briefed in media hyperbole manipulating men and excessive knowledge of the game. Much as though I would like the opportunity to lead you I think the challenge is fraught with complications.

I would have to move house and my gardener suffers from car sickness. The good agents live in London. Also I couldn't visit Ken Bates Dairy Farm to buy the yogurt or attend the Irving Scholar financial seminars. A mutual Manager and friend has reminded me that you don't have an airport so I can avail myself to the Duty Free whiskey.

I hope I haven't transmitted any doubts;I would like to leave the door open and I suppose the lure of your lira could influence me.

May I wish you good luck in your dream. Please treat this reply in absolute confidence if you retain any.

Yours sincerely,

David Pleat

David Pleat

P.S. Cesar Menotti rang me this morning he might be interested in the vacancy. He says you sound a bit South American and he was fascinated when I told him you have a cloth factory and get the Duty Free cigs.

CHARDOCK RANGERS FOOTBALL CLUB.THE ALLOTMENTS.CHARDOCK

The Greatest Football Team in the World

Police Constable Snide
The Nick
Chardock

Dear Snidey,

I trust this letter reaches you.I was given the above address but think it's incorrect as during the day your bike is outside the Dog and Duck,whilst in the evenings it seems it's constantly parked outside the front door of one of our more distinguished,and recently widowed,lady councillors.

The Two Rons will be taking over match security but I was wondering if you'd paint double yellow lines in field and pastures to prevent unauthorised parking.A set of traffic lights and a lollipop lady would also be useful,as would a couple of thousand traffic cones in the club colours of yellow and white.

I thank you for your help in this matter,if not in the previous matter regarding cheap watches,when I found you particularly unhelpful.

Yours faithfully,

Maurice Millionaire

Maurice Millionaire
Citizen
Chardock Rangers Football Club.

CHARDOCK POLICE STATION

and 24 hour dry cleaning

Mr Maurice Millionaire
(and may we say the name rings a bell)
Chardock Rangers Football Club,
The Allotments,
Chardock

Dear Maurice Millionaire,

It's a fair cop Millionaire,my bike is often parked outside the lady councillors abode but its only circumstantial evidence,it'll never hold up in court.Alright,How much ??

Regarding the traffic cones and yellow line markings in the fields,I suggest you ask your drinking chums when they leave the Dog and Duck at closing time,which last night I notice was 3.30 am,and I*d nicked the lot of you if I hadn't been pissed.

For crowd control I think the idea of inviting the Two Rons is fine and I'm sure you'll receive a favourable reply from Hale and Pace.

I expect to see you on Wednesday at 11.15 as I do every week at that time.

Yours faithfully,

PC Snide
Chardock Police
(Wrongful arrests quotations available upon request)

EARLY CLOSING ON WEDNESDAYS * CRIME PREVENTION A SPECIALITY * PLUMBING

CHARDOCK RANGERS FOOTBALL CLUB.THE ALLOTMENTS.CHARDOCK.DORSET

The Greatest Football Team in the World

The Two Rons
Hale and Pace
London Weekend Television

Dear Two Rons,

Any chance of sorting out our crowd at home matches ?

Yours faithfully

Maurice Millionaire
Chardock Rangers Football Club

International Artistes Limited
Mezzanine Floor, 235 Regent Street, London, W1R 8AX
Tel: 071 439 8401/2/3/4/5, Fax: 071 409 2070, Telex: 295061 INTART G

Please reply to:-

Wellard Mansions
Ard Street
LONDON
E1

Mr Maurice Millionaire
Chairman
Chardock Rangers F. C.
The Allotments
Chardock
Dorset

5th August 1991

Dear Maurice Millionaire,

Piss Off.

Yours,

Ron and X

Ron + Ron

P.S. We know where you live.

CHARDOCK RANGERS FOOTBALL CLUB.THE ALLOTMENTS.CHARDOCK

The Greatest Football Team in the World

Desmond Lynam
BBC Television
England

Dear Desmond Lynam,

No doubt you have heard through the TV grapevine that you were not short-listed for match day, public address commentary at Chardock.However,there is still a vacancy for carrying jackpot numbers at half time.

Your task would be to carry the results board around the ground,car parks,pubs and shops during the interval,which can be made as long as you wish.

I must ask,before you accept this post, to give some thought to your rather laid-back style which doesn suit our high profile approach.When I watched you on telly last week I thought you'd actually passed away whilst commentating on an admittedly boring item when girls,in formation,and with sickening grins,try to drown themselves.

Cheer up mate.Before reading out the results from that noisy teleprinter thing,please get very excited when you slip in the Chardock result.Perhaps the score flashing on and off with little dancing men waving and cheering. Just a thought.

Yours faithfully,

Maurice Millionaire

Maurice Millionaire
Chardock Rangers Football Club.

EXTENSION:
DIRECT LINE:
FAX:

BRITISH BROADCASTING CORPORATION
KENSINGTON HOUSE
RICHMOND WAY, LONDON W14 0AX
TELEPHONE: 081-895 6611
TELEX: 265781
CABLES: TELECASTS, LONDON

MAURICE MILLIONAIRE
CHARDOCK RANGERS FOOTBALL CLUB
THE ALLOTMENTS
CHARDOCK

25TH SEPTEMBER 1991

Dear Maurice,

At last the real reason for my switch from Grandstand to Sportsnight is out in the open.

Believe me, with the money that the BBC pay, I need that display board job, I don't beg, but will if you insist.

Yours sincerely

DESMOND LYNAM

CHARDOCK RANGERS FOOTBALL CLUB,THE ALLOTMENTS,CHARDOCK.DORSET.

The Greatest Fotball Team in the World.

Saint John.
Saint and Greavesie
ITV Sport.

Dear Saint John,

Would you be so kind as to bless our ground when we qualify for next season's European Cup Final ?

I also understand you have your own ambulance brigade ? You must be very well thought of and very rich.To that end,we are very similar,and I am certain there must be some sort of position here at Chardock Rangers which you may find suitable. Due to religious reasons,we only play on Tuesdays.Will this suit ? I await your reply with great expectancy as,I assume,did the animals on the ark.

Yours faithfully,

Maurice Millionaire
Chardock Rangers Football Club and ex choir boy.

Independent Television Sport

London Weekend Television
South Bank Television Centre London SE1 9LT

Telephone: 071-620 1620 Telex: 8811635 Fax: 071-633 0485

26th October, 1991

Mr. Maurice Millionaire,
Chardock Rangers Football Club,
The Allotments,
Chardock,
Dorset.

Dear Mr. Millionaire,

Re your letter regarding religious ceremonies at your Stadium, might I suggest that you have mistaken me for EX-BBC Sports Presenter David Icke.

As you are aware, he believes himself to be the Son of God, so I do not think that you can find anyone higher in the ecclesiastical hierachy than this gentleman. If he does accept your invitation, he could feed your crowd with five loaves and three fishes, as I gather this is about the size of your home gate.

As far as the Ambulance is concerned, I am no relation to The St.John who, apart from the Brigades, also has put his name to many Schools and Churches throughout the country, as well as a Wood in North London.

Yours sincerely,

Ian St John

IAN ST. JOHN

PS. I hope you can persuade my partner to play for you as he badly needs the exercise.

Additional thoughts of Chairman Mo.....

When it came to the electing of club president,I,Maurice Millionaire was at a loss.I knew of only a handful of Presidents in the whole World and I didn't fancy my chances at securing their services.I headhunted the two World leaders with the most clout,not only for their role at the club,but there was every chance they could lay their hands on some bloody good raffle prizes.

Sadly,neither Presidemt Mikhail Gorbachev nor President George Bush of the United States of America replied to the carefully scribed invitations.Perhaps the addresses were too vague,well who DOES know the postcode of the Kremiln for God's sake?

My only remaining option was a letter to the Prime Minister Mr John Major,asking if he could assist in this important matter,after all,Mr Major's was an office which dealt with these distant lands every day.

I felt that if the Prime Minister could not help me I was snookered,though word began to filter back that Mr Gorbachev was an ardent fan of Moscow Dynamo.I could go no higher though I appreciated he was a busy man.

Someone suggested,in the Dog and Duck,that I contact Jimmy Saville an idea which was met with the contempt it deserved when we dragged the guilty man down the A35 in a barrel of scrumpy until we arrived at Lower Smellditch whereby he was forced to view on video an entire series of 'French Fields' without a bucket.

The letter was posted in August and I awaited a reply with little hope.

Reply from the Prime Minister

And so it was on August 14th,1991,an envelope winged its way through the post with 10,Downing Street,emblazened across the back of the envelope.

It has always been source of bewilderment to me that our leader has to live in a terraced house whilst the American chap has that big White House and important Russians live in the Kremlin,well they used to anyway, and there's our poor Prime Minister,having to keep the music down because the Chancellor of the Exchequor next door is working on the budget.

I digress,the reply came from Press Secretary Jonathan Haslam,who informed me after a diary meeting with the Prime Minister,his heavy schedule did not allow him to worry about the fortunes of Chardock Rangers,and quite right too.I mean, if the Prime Minister was not looking after us all,then who on earth was.

I understood completely and wrote and told Mr Haslam so, taking the opportunity of thanking him for bothering to reply in the first place.

The official Downing Street paper had caused quite a stir in Chardock,once spotted by the post mistress.Petrol came down fifty pence a gallon,Alfie Shadey paid his television licence and there was talk of my good self standing for Parliament.

Chapter Four

The Players (sort of)

This Chapter will make you cry.

ERNIE 'TACTICS' DIXON

Captain and half brother of manager Nudger.Ernie was the originator of the innovative 3-4-4-7 formation that earned the club a record fine and points deduction in the 1960's. Ernie has trouble remembering names,specially his own,and he joined the club in 1971 from neighbouring Dormouth in a straight swap for a bag of slug pellets and a crisp.
He doesn't remember playing for Dormouth (or Chardock).

LEN 'DIXIE' DEAN

Len once pursued his mentor and namesake,Dixie Dean's record of 60 goals in a season,but agonisingly fell just 58 short.He is the main striker but has sadly not scored for Chardock for 17 years,though we all feel he should come good again very soon.He does however appear regularly in the own goals columns and has won numerous man of the match awards for opposing teams
He became a regular viewing target for pantomime agents last season and his home performances earned him the part of a tree in Chardock Musical Society's gripping production of South Pacific.
His sporting ambition is still to swim the Channel longways.

DEGSY 'SIR STANLEY' BIGGS

Razor sharp,incisive,finely tuned football brain with amazing flair,intuition,vision,perception and dazzling technical brilliance.Unfortunately he doesn't have any legs.

LEONARDO SALVADOR MARIO DI VICENTE NASIMENTO?THE NAWAB OF CHARDOCK

The club's only overseas player and most expensive signing,he is the son of a Patagonian Sheep Dipper and merchant banker. The Nawab moved to Chardock 35 years ago and became adopted by the club after late night heavy drinking sessions in the Dog and Duck.He speaks no English,has no interest in football, and has never been seen at the ground or heard of since.

DINKY BATES

At six and a half stone soaking wet and four feet eleven tall in platform boots,Dinky Bates tends to struggle with crosses above pitch level,and has an irritating habit of cadging fags off opposing forwards in return for ignoring back passes.
He should have played for England,according to the Welsh,and he remains the only player in the junior Dorset league for being sent off for being pissed.

ERNIE 'GONZALES' DREDGE

Ernie recorded the latest ever late foul when he took out a winger 3 minutes and forty seconds after he'd passed him,and two minutes after the final whistle.Encouragingly he has cut down to 75 fags a day (73 during a match) but still enjoys his yard of scotch at half time.He also plays in civvies to ensure a prompt getaway for opening time at the Dog and Duck,and to this same end,Dredgy does not play away games.His ambition is to meet his wife on 'Blind Date'.

LOFTY BEAUMONT

***Although nicknamed** Lofty,he is of normal height...but lives in the loft,due to his wife's preference for manager Nudger Dixon.He models his game on George Best by occasionally turning up and unfortunately missed all of last season through a training injury after a team mate slipped a medicine ball through his legs from 80 yards.His religious beliefs prevent his availability on weekdays.*

Not a bad collection I thought.not a bad collection at all, but deep down I had this nagging doubt that perhaps they weren't quite good enough to conquer Europe,lets face it we all know how unsporting some of those chaps can be.Plus the fact there were only seven of us.New recruits were needed and quickly.There was little time to waste,so soon the steam was rising from the typewriter once again.

Chardock Rangers Football Club, The Allotments, Chardock, Dorset.

The Greatest Football Team In The World

Headed Notepaper Not Budgeted for at Present

Gary Lineker,
Tottenham Hotspur Football Club,
748 High Road,
Tottenham,
London N17

Dear Gary Lineker,

As one of England's greatest players, according to my son, I'd like to enquire if you're available to turn out for Chardock Rangers next season as we search for World Soccer domination. We have a vacancy for a goal keeper and the big bloke at the back who heads away the corners.

Unfortunately we have no money but can offer you a mobile home time share for the last week in October and the first in November, and a sponsored club moped.

I appreciate you are busy on Saturday with those Spurs, but we intend to play on Tuesday afternoons when it doesn't clash with skittles, or Tuesday evenings if we can get a team.

Perhaps you can drop me a line as I've already leaked your possible arrival to the Chardock Herald and most of us are looking forward to seeing you playing in our yellow and white striped shirts and brown shorts, by the way, I've just been on to that Subbuteo chap to find out why he doesn't make those little men in those particular colours.

If we achieve soccer domination as I suspect we shall in Europe, would you be able to read out the team changes in Spanish ?

Thanking you in anticipation. I look forward to your reply.

Yours faithfully,

Maurice Millionaire
Chardock Rangers Football Club.

Gary Lineker
Tottenham Hotspur Football & Athletic Co. Ltd.
748 High Road, Tottenham, London N17 0AP

Dear Mr Millionaire

I thank you for your recent offer. You must be the Mr Millionaire who sold me a new Rolls Royce last year. I now understand that this was in fact a counterfeit and it requires an MOT certificate.

I will not consider your offer until I receive the same.

Yours faithfully,

[signature]

CHARDOCK RANGERS FOOTBALL CLUB.THE ALLOTMENTS.CHARDOCK

The Greatest Football Team in the World

Mr Billy Wright
Wolverhampton Wanderers

Dear Billy Wright,

It is a great privilige to write to a legend such as yourself.The way you flew the Atlantic with your brother and all that.I am told you are a centre-half and team could do with a few of them.

Would you care to display your talents with Chardock Rangers next season.In so doing,you will of course enhance your prospects of adding to the large collection of hats already in your possession for representing your country.

In browsing through the Wolverhampton Wandereers team lists for last season I couldn't help noticing your name was mysteriously absent.Could you please let me know if you are injured,resting,or simply out of favour ? If you don't reply I'll assume it's probably all three and I'll cross you off my list..My cap size is 6⅞

Yours faithfully,

[signature]

Maurice Millionaire
Chardock Rangers Football Club.

Oct 7th 1991

Dear Mr Millionaire,

Thankyou for your interesting enquiry. I would like to wish Chardock Rangers the best of luck next season, but am forced to decline your offer of a place in the team, because I am at present fully occupied refereeing The Beverley Sisters.

Yours in sport.
Billy Wright
C.B.E

BILLY WRIGHT C.B.E.

CHARDOCK RANGERS FOOTBALL CLUB.THE ALLOTMENTS.CHARDOCK

The Greatest Football Team in the World

Headed notepaper due any day now

Chris and Robin Smith
Hampshire Cricket Club

Dear Chris and Robin Smith,

As you two South African chaps seem to be two of England's best batsmen,I would like to give you the opportunity of emulating the great Denis and Leslie Compton by competing in world class cricket and football.

Apparently,the Comptons played for Middlesex and Arsenal.I am delighted to offer you the chance of playing for Hampshire and Chardock Rangers.

We play on Tuesday afternoons but are prepared to offer you a tea interval of half an hour in all matches other than cup games.We cannot offer money as we're cleaned out,but would be more than pleased to accompany you to Australia and the West Indies (if you sort out the tickets.) There are 27 of us in Chardock but why not make it a round 40 and we'll get some lads from the next village to travel too. They love a drink.Chokey Chalmers is apparently the loudest farter in Dorset,and he'd be great company.

I look forward to your reply in English.

Yours faithfully,

Maurice Millionaire

Maurice Millionaire.
Chardock Rangers Football Club.

HAMPSHIRE COUNTY CRICKET CLUB

Chief Executive:
A.F. BAKER F.C.A.

Marketing Manager:
M.N.S. TAYLOR

COUNTY CRICKET GROUND
NORTHLANDS ROAD
SOUTHAMPTON S09 2TY
Telephone : 0703 - 333788
Fax : 0703 - 330121
Cricketscene
Instant Scores : 0839 - 333366
Reports : 0839 - 333365

Western Australia Cricket Association
Perth
Western Australia

Maurice Millionaire
Chardock Rangers Football Club
The Allotments
Chardock

Dear Mr Millionaire

Further to your proposition made to myself and brother Robin to join Chardock Rangers, thus emulating the successes of Denis and Leslie Compton in football and cricket, I'm afraid, as you can see by the address, I have taken up new employment in Australia and much as the offer is tempting, I'm afraid I would find the commuting both strenuous and prohibitive. If ever you're a couple of players short in your European assault, we may find we could all meet halfway, but to achieve this you will need to draw against sides from Thailand and Indonesia, quite unlikely I presume.

As for brother Robin, as you know, he is on England duty at present and once he receives your Chardock Rangers fixture list, he will ensure a cricket tour abroad is planned, even if it means him booking the thing himself, but if it weren't for that he would love to play for Chardock Rangers.

I wish you the best of luck with your World soccer domination, and should you ever require a Chardock surfing side I would be more than prepared to undertake the coaching by mail order.

With best wishes

Chris Robin

Chris and Robin Smith

BKL
SPONSORED BY
Brooking Knowles
& Lawrence
Chartered Accountants

CHARDOCK RANGERS FOOTBALL CLUB.THE ALLOTMENTS.CHARDOCK

The Greatest Football Team in the World

Alan Ball
Exeter Speedway
Devon

Dear Alan Ball,

I was astonished to discover in the lost and found columns of the Chardock Herald that you lost a pub and found a job at Exeter (Speedway I presume.)Exeter is very near Chardock (either thirty miles or ninety thousand, depending on which car you bought from me.)Why didn't you play for us ?

I gather from a reliable source in the Dog and Duck,who I'd never met before in my life,that you helped England win the World Cup,though he didn't say how.Could I suggest,to get yourself in shape for future World Cups,you turn out for Chardock.We play on Tuesday afternoons,if sheep grazing allows,so won't get in the way of your speedway.Those noisey riders upset my tropical fish.Indeed,I've had to bring the aquarium indoors.

When you reply,due to your age,please enclose a medical certificate.A decent forgery will suffice.

Yours faithfully,

Maurice Millionaire
Chardock Rangers Football Club

EXETER CITY FOOTBALL CLUB

St. James' Park, Exeter EX4 6PX
Telephone: (0392) 54073
Fax No: (0392) 425885
Training Ground: (0395) 32784
Centre Spot Social Club: (0392) 50292

Dear Maurice,

Thanks for your offer to play with Chardock Rangers.

At this moment in time I am managing the above named Club but by the time this letter gets to you I may not be!! Things happen quick to managers you know!!

As you are well aware Exeter have the same fixture dates as Chardock but as the players take no notice of me what so ever they would not miss me.

My only stipulation in coming to play for you is that you do not take the micky out of my voice and I can have a few bob to go racing with Maurice.

Please reply quickly as I am putting weight on by the day.

Yours sincerely,

Alan Ball.

P.S. In your reply could you enclose race fixtures for Devon & Exeter and Newton Abbot.

CHARDOCK RANGERS FOOTBALL CLUB.THE ALLOTMENTS.CHARDOCK

The Greatest Football Team in the World

Liam Brady
Celtic Football Club.
Scotland.

Dear Liam Brady,

I understand for some reason which escapes me, you spent some time playing in Italy.I assume you must have, at some stage,met up with that South African lad Diego Madonna. I'm interested in bringing him to Chardock Rangers,provided he pays his own expenses.Do you have his home telephone number ? On second thoughts get him to phone me,as I don't have the code for Italy.

Thank you for your help in this matter.

Yours faithfully,

Maurice Millionaire
Chardock Rangers Football Club.

The Celtic Football and Athletic Company Ltd.

VAT Reg. No. 260 2974 61 | Registered Office, Celtic Park, Glasgow G40 3RE | Registered No. 3487 Scotland

CELTIC PARK,
GLASGOW G40 3RE

Tel: 041-554 2710

Caro Milliardario

Mi Dispiace ma non posso aiutare. Credo che Diego adesso è a Buenos Aires e io so il numero.

[signature]

Manager Celtic F.C.

Footnote from Maurice Millionaire;
'Why did Liam Brady reply in Scottish?'

CHARDOCK RANGERS FOOTBALL CLUB.THE ALLOTMENTS.CHARDOCK

The Greatest Football Team in the World

Tony Gale
West Ham United
Upton Park.

Dear Tony Gale,

In my quest to make Chardock Rangers the greatest team in the world,it has occured to me our current side is crap. In a recent FA Cup semi-final between Nottingham Forset and West Ham,I named you 'man of the match'.How sad it was they slung you off after a few minutes.However,the speed at which you left the field proved to me you could fit in well with our style of play,with Lofty Beaumont the only current player who could possibly keep up with you.

We intend to play on Tuesday afternoons so this will not interfere with West Ham duties.We cannot pay any money but can offer you a caravan the last week in November,as a time share.You'd have to share with Vinny Jones if we sign him. Let us know what you think.

Yours faithfully,

Maurice Millionaire
Chardock Rangers Football Club.

Telephone: 081-472 2740
Facsimile No.: 081-471 2997

West Ham United Football Co., Ltd.

Company Registration No. 66516 Registered in England
V.A.T. Registration No. 248 5000 77

Secretary:
T. M. FINN

Team Manager:
BILLY BONDS, M.B.E.

REGISTERED OFFICE:
BOLEYN GROUND
GREEN STREET
UPTON PARK
LONDON, E13 9AZ

Your Ref. ....

Our Ref. ....

Dear Maurice

Unfortunately I am contracted to West Ham for the next 3 seasons and have to decline your generous offer of joining Charrack Rangers.

If in 3 seasons time you are still interested in me, is it possible to sign a contract whereby I could play for just 30 minutes as I just couldn't trust myself to last the full 90 minutes with this new proffessional foul ruling. An honest tug push or trip always seems to be misinterpreted by these stupid refs!

Telephone: 081-472 2740
Facsimile No.: 081-471 2997

West Ham United Football Co., Ltd.

Company Registration No. 66516 Registered in England
V.A.T. Registration No. 248 5000 77

Secretary:
T. M. FINN

Team Manager:
BILLY BONDS, M.B.E.

REGISTERED OFFICE:
BOLEYN GROUND
GREEN STREET
UPTON PARK
LONDON, E13 9AZ

Your Ref. ....

Our Ref. ....

P.S. The incentive of the time share seems to be particularly generous, (shame about the company) as we haven't picked up many bonuses at West Ham lately.

Yours sincerely

Tony Gale

CHARDOCK RANGERS FOOTBALL CLUB.THE ALLOTMENTS.CHARDOCK

The Greatest Football Team in the World

Peter Reid
Manchester City FC

Dear Peter Reid,

Did my eyes deceive me or was that really you I saw playing for Manchester City the other week ?

According to Charlie Buchan's Football Annual, you were a seasoned campaigner in 1951,yet there you were chasing footballers a quarter your age and,in one case,nearly catching one.Such enthusiasm,however misguided,is just what we need at Chardock Rangers.I was thinking perhaps you could play the first eight minutes and then sell hot dogs around the ground.

Could you also bring some of those striking wigs you wear,those grey ones,as they'd be useful on Halloween at the Dog and Duck.

I look forward to hearing from you in the near future and should you play for us,you will be our youngest player by eleven years.

Yours faithfully,

Maurice Millionaire
Chardock Rangers Football Club

TELEPHONE Nº 061-226 1191/2
FAX Nº 061-227 9418

TELEGRAPHIC ADDRESS: "FOOTBALL MANCHESTER 14"

MANCHESTER CITY FOOTBALL CLUB PLC

REGISTERED IN ENGLAND REGISTERED NUMBER 40946

REGISTERED OFFICE & GROUND
MAINE ROAD
MOSS SIDE
MANCHESTER
M14 7WN

WINNERS EUROPEAN CUP WINNERS CUP 1970
WINNERS F.A. CHALLENGE CUP 1904, 1934, 1956, 1969
FINALISTS F.A. CHALLENGE CUP 1926, 1933, 1955, 1981
LEAGUE (1ST DIVISION) CHAMPIONS 1937, 1968
RUNNERS-UP 1904, 1921, 1977
WINNERS FOOTBALL LEAGUE CUP 1970, 1976
LEAGUE (2ND DIVISION) CHAMPIONS 1899, 1903, 1910, 1928, 1947, 1966
RUNNERS-UP 1896, 1951, 1989
CENTRAL LEAGUE CHAMPIONS 1978, 1987
WINNERS F.A. YOUTH CUP 1986
FULL MEMBERS CUP FINALISTS 1986
FINALISTS FOOTBALL LEAGUE CUP 1974

PR/JMcC

Mr M Millionaire
Chardock Rangers Football Club
The Allotments
Chardock
Dorset

Dear Mr Millionaire,

It took me a little time to come back down to earth after receiving your letter. To say that I feel honoured to be asked to play for you is an understatement - but to sell hot dogs around the ground as well can only mean that I will have reached the pinnacle of my career!

I have spent sleepless nights over this decision - I can only describe my dilemma as the hardest decision I have had to make in my long career in football.

In my heart I know that I should say "yes", but as Manager/ Player of Manchester City I have a commitment to keep, therefore it is with the greatest of regrets that I am compelled to say "no" to you.

However, all is not lost - I will forward to you a few of the grey wigs you admired - you should receive them in time for Halloween. Please give my very best wishes to everyone at the Dog and Duck.

My very best wishes to you, Mr Millionaire, and once again my heartfelt thanks for the kind offer you made me.

Yours sincerely,

Peter Reid

PETER REID
Manager

Telephone: **081-472 2740**
Facsimile No.: **081-471 2997**

West Ham United Football Co., Ltd.

Company Registration No. 66516 Registered in England
V.A.T. Registration No. 248 5000 77

Secretary:
T. M. FINN

Team Manager:
BILLY BONDS, M.B.E.

REGISTERED OFFICE:
BOLEYN GROUND
GREEN STREET
UPTON PARK
LONDON, E13 9AZ

Your Ref. ....

Our Ref. ....

To Maurie Millionaire,

Get off my back!
George Parris
GEORGE PARRIS.

Get lost!
Steve Potts
STEVE POTTS.

Piss off!
Matthew Rush
MATTHEW RUSH.

No way!
TIM BREACKER

Leave me alone!
STUART SLATER.

On your bike!
IAN BISHOP.

CHARDOCK RANGERS FOOTBALL CLUB.THE ALLOTMENTS.CHARDOCK

The Greatest Football Team in the World

Paul Gascoigne
A Football Club
Europe

Dear Gazza,

I won't take up your time as you're probably reading this perched on one leg,but should you feel the need to extend your football playing boundaries to deepest Dorset,please do not hesitate to contact me at Chardock Rangers.

I'm sick to death of the way the press hound you.You'll be safe down here.Indeed,our local Constable Snide thinks you're brilliant on University Challenge and would give you a quiet life (which is more than he gives me.)

If you manage to reply I'll have to include further along the book as those cheeky West Ham chaps have blagged yours.

Yours faithfully,

Maurice Millionaire
Chardock Rangers Football Club.

CHARDOCK RANGERS FOOTBALL CLUB.THE ALLOTMENTS.CHARDOCK

The Greatest Football Team in the World

Headed notepaper not declared

Mark Nicholas
Hampshire Cricket Club

Dear Mark Nicholas,

I have followed your career since you came down fom Celtic.Those wonderful goals you scored for Arsenal,and then Aberdeen,and then....nothing.

Suddenly,I'm watching Hampshire as my 19th prize in a Reader's Digest draw,when I spot this long haired chap by the name of Nicholason the boundary with a hip flask and a walkman.I think the music was Jimmy Shand's greatest hits. Come back to football Charlie........relive those halcyon days with Chardock Rangers.We play on Tuesday afternoons and we have great New Year's Eve parties every Thursday.

By the way,if you know Moira Anderson,we're still looking for someone to lead the community singing.What do you think Jimmy ? Och aye the noo.

Yours faithfully,

Maurice MacMillionaire
Chardock Rangers Football Club.

Maurice Millionaire,
Chardock Rangers,
The Allotments,
Chardock
Dorset.

Dear Maurice Millionaire,

I was completely amazed to hear that you were back in civilian life and recruiting for a football team for the coming season.

I say 'amazed' because I thought you'd still be passing your time with various jockeys and brewers.Anyway,regards your offer of playing for Chardock Rangers,get stuffed.On Tuesday afternoons I'm commited to voluntary work with the boy scouts (now that IS nice work if you can get it).

Incidentally,I don't know Moira Anderson's phone number,well at least I haven't got it with me as I'm away for the weekend performing exacting tasks for the Red Cross.

I think you've confused me with another sportsman,but please give me a call if ever you are in Southampton and come and watch us play.My hair is even longer now and I am batting even worse,but because I'm captain I keep picking myself.

Best wishes slopping out for the rest of your life.

Yours sincerely,

Mark Nicholas.

Benefit Office: Kate Dickson, 21 Canton Street, Southampton SO1 2DJ. ☎0703 630031 fax 0703 234849

Chairman: Tim Rice

Executive Chairman: Roger Treherne, 'Woodlands', Hadrian Way, Chilworth, Southampton SO1 7HY. ☎0703 767555 (Home), 0703 634333 (Office)

Treasurer: Nigel Butler, 'Stumped', Wedmans Lane, Rotherwick, Basingstoke RG27 9BS

Co-ordinators: Chris Goldie (The General), Malcolm Le Bas (Southampton), Denis Simpson (Cricket), Derek Wyatt, Simon Denehy, Tim Wright, Trevor Rudd (London)

CHARDOCK RANGERS FOOTBALL CLUB.THE ALLOTMENTS.CHARDOCK

The Greatest Football Team in the World

David O'Leary
Arsenal FC

Dear David O'Leary,

I am sure it is an oversight on your part, I do not seem to have received an application for you to play for Chardock Rangers.No doubt our letters will cross in the post.

A friend has loosely recommended you but I am not sure,from his appallingly scribbled note,if you have played seven or seven thousand games for Arsenal.We therefore require confirmation of your age,my mate estimates fifty two but admits he could be a month or two out.We also require proof of identity (Gas bill,library ticket etc.)A quick reply would be appreciated as the programme printer wants to go on holiday.

Yours faithfully,

Maurice Millionaire

Maurice Millionaire
Chardock Rangers Football Club.

TELEGRAMS: GUNNERETIC LONDON N5 TELEX: 298083 ARSNAL G.

ARSENAL FOOTBALL CLUB LTD.

Secretary: K. J. FRIAR

ARSENAL STADIUM
HIGHBURY
LONDON N5 1BU
TELEPHONE: 01-226 0304

D. O. Leary.

Dear Maurice

Thank you for your kind offer to come and Join your great club which you have so kindly told me about.

I must decline on the grounds of being a one Club Man it was a very hard choice for My Family and Myself.

Yours Sincerely

Dave O'Leary.

P.S. May I Just thank you for being so aware of my Career and the offer of A Chance to Play in Europe.

Company Registration Number 109244 England

Tottenham Hotspur Football & Athletic Co. Ltd.
MEMBERS OF FOOTBALL ASSOCIATION AND THE FOOTBALL LEAGUE

AUDERE EST FACERE

748 High Road, Tottenham N17 0AP. Telephone 081-808 8080 Telex 295261 Fax 081-885 1951
Dial - A - Seat: 081-808 3030 Answerphone: 0898-100515

HAWLEY CRESCENT
LONDON NW1 8EF
TEL: 071-267 4300
FAX: 071-267 6513

DIRECT LINE:

Dear Mr Millionaire, or may I call you Morris - or perhaps as an ex-Totteham Hotspur man, Morrie My Boy.

I was more than honoured to receive your invitation to again recapture my goal-scoring ability with my head, for which I was once well-famed. In actual fact, the last address that was given to you was correct, it still is the Salvation Army Hostel in Paddington. It is for this reason that I cannot possibly play for you, since I have to turn out for War Cry on Saturdays and of course do my stint on the tambourine in the band down the Charing Cross Road on Sundays.

I would like to correct your first sentence that the person I work with on my religious chat show is not a strange Scottish monk and would like to add that Brian Walden may interview Prime Ministers, David Frost may interview Royalty but only I talk to a Saint.

Best wishes for the coming season.

Yours sincerely

Jimmy Greaves

OF
ATLETICO
Payne

Chapter Five.....And so into Europe

Europe had been the battlefield for many years of conflict and bitter disagreement.There were the mods and rockers punch ups in Bournemouth and Margate,the Fight for Ownership of Harrods,and of course the huge fight to resist the building of the Channel Tunnel.

There was no doubt the mopeds with their left hand drive design would be of little consequence in the rues and straatsers,though it was all we had.We needed to contact an airline which would accomodate them and a hotel which would keep their eye on them,God knows,there's enough joy-riders around these days.

Baggagefor carrying our togs to the corners of the Continent, language obstacles,after all,few of our players spoke English, Nudger Dixon did nothing more than grunt,and that was only when he was constipated.

Letters,some air mail in pretty blue paper,were left with the postmistress at Chardock Post Office,to fly in great haste to the parties concerned,though how long this would all take was of course debatable as Mrs Grump was never known for her speedy actions.She was,after all,the woman who knitted a jumper for the 1953 Coronation and presented the one completed sleeve to Barnet Football Club to celebrate their entry into the Fourth Division.

Flying was essential,though I wouldn't necessarily admit that to a bunch of pissed up Vikings in a longboat,and so I proceeded to scribble away to those concerned,They do say that flying is the safest form of travel,I agree but I can't ever recall these people sitting in the back of my wife's car.But that's another story......

PORTSMOUTH

FOOTBALL COMPANY LIMITED

Registered Office:
FRATTON PARK, PORTSMOUTH, HANTS. PO4 8RA
Tel: 731204

For the attention of;
Mr Maurice Millionaire,
Club Chairman,
Chardock Rangers Football Club,
The Allotments,
Chardock,
Dorset.

Dear Mr Millionaire,

With reference to your telephone call this afternoon, I can confirm that Horatio Nelson is not a member of Portsmouth Supporters Club, as a matter of fact Viscount Nelson died in 1805 and it therefore seems unlikely he could assist you with Crossing the Channel when Chardock Rangers play in Europe.

Referring once again to your telephone message it seems that British Midlands Airways could be the answer.

We wish Chardock Rangers the very best of luck in their forthcoming European campaign.

Yours sincerely,

J. M. Smith

Portsmouth Football Club.

Chardock Rangers Football Club,The Allotments,Chardock,Dorset

The Greatest Football Team in the World

Headed notepaper awaiting Royal Approval.

The Shop Manager
Harrods
Brompton Road,
London SW8

Dear Sir,

Following our telephone conversation this afternoon which you chose to cut short saying you had a customer walk in,I didn't seem to receive a reply from you regarding the possibility of borrowing a couple of your largest hampers to carry our football kit through Europe next season.

When I was a lad,I had a Saturday job at Chardock's butchers and so I know how busy you all get,but I found it a little hard to take when you left me holding on for four and a quarter hours,only to be told to ring the following day as it was early closing.Our local butcher's up to his ears flogging turkeys at Christmas but he always apparantly finds the time to discuss the best way of stuffing with the local housewives.Indeed,even PC Snide has taken a great interest in the matter.

So listen,it was only a civil question and you won't become a successful store if you don't show a little civility and goodwill.

I will get back to British Midland and tell them not to worry about a roof rack as I'm telling the lads to wear their kit on the plane.

Yours faithfully,

Maurice Millionaire

CHARDOCK RANGERS FOOTBALL CLUB.THE ALLOTMENTS.CHARDOCK

The Greatest Football Team in the World

The Holiday Inn
Gatwick Airport.
Sussex

Dear Sir,

With the continuing success of our football club,it is highly likely that very soon we'll be in the finals of the European Cup.

I am undertaking preliminary enquiries regarding travel arrangements to clubs abroad,and as we have little money, I was wondering if you have two rooms available,one with five beds and one with six ?

Do you have railings round your hotel so we can padlock our mopeds on them while we are abroad ?

Yours faithfully,

Maurice Millionaire
Chardock Rangers Football Club.

HOLIDAY INN LONDON - GATWICK
Langley Drive - Crawley - West Sussex RH11 7SX - England - Tel.: 0293-529991 - Fax: 0293-515913 - Holidex: GWCUK

Mr Maurice Millionaire
Chardock Rangers FC
The Allotments
Chardock
Dorset.

Dear Mr Millionaire,

Thank you for your letter.Unfortunately we cannot meet your requirements at this particular hotel as we have no rooms containing five or six beds,and railings around our perimeter are a thing of the past.

I am sorry we are unable to help on this particular occasion but hope we can be of assistance in the future.

We at the Holiday Inn wish your football Club the very best of luck in Europe and we assure you of our best attention at all times.

Yours faithfully,

Holiday Inn
Gatwick Airport.

CHARDOCK RANGERS FOOTBALL CLUB.THE ALLOTMENTS.CHARDOCK

The Greatest Football team in the World

Headed notepaper accidentally shredded during lunchtime drink

General Sales Manager
British Midland Airways

Dear Graham Hunter,

I am having difficulty in storing our sponsored club mopeds within the vicinity of a major airport. I therefore am enquiring if you have any aircraft in your current fleet with roofracks?

If not,as we enter the away stages of the European Cup,would you be able to fly us to the stadiums, circle while we play and then bring us home ?If you can confirm this I will take the matter further by discussing long term repayment schemes.I trust,by the way,you sell duty free scrumpy ?

Should you wish to visit us at Chardock we have a very long field which,although bearing a fine crop of turnips this year,would be quite adequate for landing your company plane.I await your call.

Yours faithfully,

Marvin Millin

Wing Commander Millionaire
Chardock Rangers Football Club.

British Midland
Donington Hall
Castle Donington
Derby DE7 2SB

Telephone Derby (0332) 810741
International +44 (332) 810741
Fax (0332) 852662
Telex 37172 BMAOBD G
Sita EMAOOBD

Mr Maurice Millionaire
Chardock Rangers F.C
The Allotments
Chardock
Dorset

Our ref:
Your ref:

31st July 1991

Dear Mr Millionaire,

Many thanks for your recent letter. I wish you every success on your quest to enter European competition next year. We as a Company can relate to this ambition, as in recent years within our industry we have taken on the 'Big Boys' of Europe with remarkable success.

Your request does however present us with some problems. We could store your sponsored mopeds near an airport, but only at NCP rates. Also none of our current fleet carry roof racks, but we could store them in the hold subject to the required safety standards, eg. the draining of all two-stoke from the tanks, and the deflation of the tyres (assuming they are not of the solid variety!).

I am sure we could accommodate you in flying your team to the required destinations, and suggest you contact our Charter Department who would advise you of the relevant costs. Currently we do not stock any alcoholic, apple derivative beverages on board, but we have reacted to the suggestion and have conducted extensive research and test sampling.

I would be happy to visit you and discuss the matter further, but I would be travelling by car as your turnip encrusted landing strip could do untold damage to our Company plane.

In conclusion I regret that this is largely a negative response. I am sure however that we could at least discuss ourselves taking some pitch-side advertising space, and possibly an advertising slot in your match programmes.

Myself and British Midland wish you every possible future success.

Yours sincerely

G Hunter

Graham Hunter
General Sales Manager

CHARDOCK RANGERS FOOTBALL CLUB.THE ALLOTMENTS.CHARDOCK

The Greatest Football Team in the World

David Gunson
Air Traffic Controller
Birmingham Airport

Dear David Gunson,

I spotted your name on a door I was ducking past by the customs desk at Birmingham Airport the other week.It occured to me you may well be the man to help us with some information we require for our European Cup travel.

Some of my players are a little worried about being late back from abroad and missing important skittles matches. We require a timetable of flight delays.Would you also tell that stroppy customs official that where I live in Chardock,lots of people wear watches on their legs and under their socks.Besides, I was about to ring him anyway.
Oh yes,and what is an Air Traffic Controller and how big are they ?

Yours faithfully,

Bomber Millionaire
Chardock Rangers Football Club.

PS. Sorry it's not typed.

SAFETY IN THE AIR.

Dear MR Millionaire chappy,

Many thanks for your letter and may I be the first to congratulate you and your club on your return to European Competition. I read of your previous visit in an old parchment and the team are to be congratulated for a sparkling display marred only by the Pheonicians scoring forty eight goals. - I also read the journey to the collisseum was difficult after one of Hannibel's elephant had stood on the goal-keeper foot.

Reference your flight this year, please put all your troubles in your old kit-bag and with reasonable good fortune they will be flown to any part of the word other than the one stated on your ticket.

Delays I am pleased to say are minimal since a new system tried by our amigos in Spain has now been accepted world-wide, delays upto eight hours do not count, eight to sixteen are small, sixteen to twenty-four are short and over twenty four hours your ticket is deemed to be invalid.

I have passed your photo's on to customs and they advise not packing your luggage too neatly and don't bother to lock them, Also please destroy or burn dirty washing as it leads to embarassment when displayed in the customs hall.

Yours moved to tears.

D.R. Gunson

D.R. GUNSON

CHARDOCK RANGERS FOOTBALL CLUB.THE ALLOTMENTS.CHARDOCK

The Greatest Football Team in the World

Peter Brackley
British Sky Broadcasting

Dear Peter Brackley,

Firstly,due to the cost of typewriter ribbons, may I suggest you find employment with a company that has a shorter address.Secondly,I require your assistance.

Due to flight problems and the fact our team is crap,our European campaign is on a downward spiral at the moment.As the man who does those frightfully boring commentaries in countries all over the place.We've been at war with most of them. Is there any chance you could help me save face by showing a video of an old game where a side with yellow and white striped shirts and brown shorts wins.Then substitute their players for ours on your commentary.I'm prepared to offer you a partnership in my second hand car business and an invite to the wedding of Bill Wyman to my great grandaughter.

This year has been disastrous for Chardock.To have you commentate one of our games would be the icing on the cake.I await your reply.

Yours faithfully,

Maurice Millionaire

Maurice Millionaire
Chardock Rangers Football Club.

To;Maurice Millionaire
Chardock Rangers Football Club,
The Allotments,
Chardock,
Dorset.

Dear Maurice,

Many thanks for your interesting letter of eight months ago and how pleased I am that they finally let you out.I have unfortunately been out of the country of late, covering the mixed and men's over 50,5 a side,or was it the over 5's,50 a side (any way who gives a stuff) in Mogadishu.I replied before I left but somehow the letter seems to have found its way back to my in-tray via an over zealous cleaning lady who thought that screwed up paper should be recycled rather than thrown away.

Anyway,unfortunately,despite many hours if not minutes of meticulous searching through our archives,alright, a phone call,I have been unable to unearth any teams wearing yellow and white stripes and brown shorts,or indeed any permutations thereof in squares,stripes,hoops,spots,nasty smears or wedding dresses.I have though found film of a team in yellowwho play in the far distant wastes of East Anglia. The particular game is a muddy affair and I hope this shall suffice.

Could you be so kind as to send me a list of your players' names so I can practise getting them wrong for my commentary?Naturally,as a keen follower of football,I have heard ofand indeed long since admired,Ernie Dredge,but with the exception of boss Nudger Dixon who did a particularly stunning interview on television last week......Crimewatch if I recall correctly,some of your other star players are not familiar to me.Particularly your overseas internationals. For instance,I gather from a contact that someone called Rosie is a damn good sport,Is that short for Rosenblatt,Rosenthal or Rosenbärg perhaps,Apparantly I hear Rosie has no problem making the first eleven,though what my contact meant by 'And some of the reserve side too...' I don't quite follow.

I would prefer not to dabble in your second hand car business as means of payment,andas for Bill Wyman's wedding. I think I'll pass on that too until one of my own relations are perhaps involved.

May I take this opportunity of wishing Chardock Rangers the very best of luck in Europe,and with your good self at the helm they should go a long way,as I seem to recall you once did in the back of an ambulance.

With best wishes,
Yours sincerely,

P. Brackley

Peter Brackley
Sky Television.

Some European Campaign this could turn out to be. It only proved to me the grim determination of people like Adolf Hitler, Louis Napoleon and Katie Boyle smiling through the eternal lifespan of the Eurovision Song Contest

Was World domination actually worth all this grief ? As an unwanted child I always became bored halfway through a game of Monopoly and I sensed the same seaping of interest from a man who only wanted the best for Chardock Rangers. Sometimes it makes you wonder who won the bloody war in the first place.

Happily for me, the players were enthusiastic as ever and before too long they had enrolled at a nearby Technical College, as instructed by me, to assist in our quest for the European Cup. One studied languages, the others woodwork, thus ensuring a boat ride across the Channel as a last resort. It was never this complicated in the Dorset Unskilled League for the Elderly, and somehow I have a gut feeling that perhaps at that level our fortunes lie.

Image, that's what we lacked. We needed class projection to make people sit up and take notice. Then we could start a supporter's club, interest the media, sell the rights and generally be in the running for a fair wedge of dosh.

Just one additional sentence and I felt rejuvinated. The children of tomorrow should be flicking Chardock Subbuteo players alongside the Real Madrids and Barcelonas. Supporters in their own luxury coaches with onboard videos of Helga and her friendly farmyard friends.

We just HAD to get into Europe. I just HAD to get to Sweden

Chapter Six.......A touch of Class.....Image

CHARDOCK RANGERS FOOTBALL CLUB.THE ALLOTMENTS.CHARDOCK.

The Greatest Football Team in the World

Headed notepaper not printed due to lack of patron

Graham Taylor
Manager
England Football Club
England

Dear Graham Taylor,

It was news to me and the other regulars in the Dog and Duck,when midway through Saturday's darts match against the Fatted Cow,one of their lot let slip that Alf Ramsey's packed it in at England.Is that right you're in charge ?

You will want to know the potential of possible aspiring internationals at Chardock Rangers.To save you the trouble of coming down,I wouldn't bother.The team is crap.In return for such honesty is there any chance you can use your clout and fix us a friendly with Brazil? Any Tuesday at the end of October will be fine,and if they play skittles,we'll chuck a few woods down in the evening.

Will you tell them we only do tea after the game so if they want that instant stuff they'll have to bring their own.Thanks mate,and should you ever want to put England through their paces at skittles cart them down here.

Yours faithfully

Maurice Millionaire
Chardock Rangers Football Club.

THE FOOTBALL ASSOCIATION
LIMITED
Founded 1863

Patron: HER MAJESTY THE QUEEN
President: H.R.H. THE DUKE OF KENT
Chairman: SIR BERT MILLICHIP

Chief Executive:
R. H. G. KELLY FCIS

Phone: 071-402 7151/071-262 4542
Telex: 261110
Facsimile: 071-402 0486

16 LANCASTER GATE, LONDON W2 3LW

Our Ref: *Your Ref:*

Maurice Millionaire
Chardock Rangers Football Club
The Allotments
Chardock
Dorset

Dear Mr Millionaire

Thank you for your recent letter.

Your dart opponents at the "Fatted Cow" are just a little bit way behind the times - in fact something like a quarter of a century - and as well as Sir Alf Ramsey no longer being the England Manager there are somewhat other small changes in life such as decimalisation and entry to the European Community Still these are small matters and I suppose to the dedicated dart thrower they can - like double top - be easily missed.

I am pleased you have told me about the quality of your team, but quite honestly it appears to be no different from the teams that I have managed throughout my career and certainly must be on par with my present one.

As regards your request for a friendly game with Brazil, can you remember the name of the coloured chap who played in the number ten shirt during the sixties? The reason I am asking is that for all the publicity he got - and what do the press know about it anyhow! - he never gave me the impression that he had any rhythm or real ability. In fact I think that the greater majority of the thousand goals that he scored during his career were plain lucky. He certainly would not have been able to pass any knowledge of playing skittles down to the present team and because of that what is the point of inviting them for a friendly?

Can you also imagine them bringing their own coffee. I mean how are you going to crush the beans. No it seems to me Chairman that it would be much better if the England team came down and played the game of skittles that you suggest.

I can see why you are a Millionaire because I think that it is your intention to introduce floodlit games of skittles on full size football pitches thereby bringing back the natural aggression to our game which FIFA through their pansid amendments are destroying. Many congratulations on your foresight!

Yours sincerely

Graham Taylor
England Team Manager

PS: Was the Brazilian called Tele? - if he had been any good I would have remembered his name.

CHARDOCK RANGERS FOOTBALL CLUB.THE ALLOTMENTS.CHARDOCK

The Greatest Football Team in the World

Headed notepaper in second class post apparently.

Trevor Spencer
Subbuteo Games
The Toy Shop
Chardock

Dear Trevor Spencer,

Since childhood Subbuteo has been,for me, the greatest game in the world.I therefore find it most distressing that word has not filtered through to you regarding the massive contribution Chardock Rangers will be making to world soccer next season.

I notice that no Subbuteo side is available in our colours of yellow and white stripes and brown shorts. Don't be caught out.I have taken the liberty of already placing an order for ten sets at the toy shop,and our smallest player,Dinky Bates and his nephew Billy 'Beanpole' Archer are on stand-by should you require models._our goalkeeper by the way wears a blue anorak with the hood up as it gets windy here on the coast.

I await your reply.

Yours faithfully,

Maurice Millionaire.
Chardock Rangers Football Club.

Subbuteo Sports Games

Castle Gate, Oulton, Leeds LS26 8HG, England
Telephone: Leeds (0532) 824961
Telex: 557421 Wadint G.
Fax:(0532) 822958

6 August 1991

Mr M Millionaire
Chardock Rangers Football Club
The Allotments
Chardock

Dear Mr Millionaire

Many thanks for your recent letter regarding the introduction of CHARDOCK RANGERS F.C. to the range of Subbuteo teams.

We have in fact been considering adding Chardock Rangers to the range for several months, as we take great pride in representing not only the teams from the lower divisions but also major clubs such as Liverpool, Arsenal, Juventus, Barcelona and Chardock Rangers. The reason for the delay in releasing the Chardock Rangers Subbuteo team is that we are waiting for confirmation of their new strip for the forthcoming season.

We are pleased to see that the Chardock Rangers kit is remaining in its traditional style of yellow and white stripes with uniquely distinctive brown shorts.

As to the goalkeeper design, we have decided to produce the Chardock goalie in an anorak (with hood up) in powder blue, this will of course complement our Faroe Isles 'Bobble Hat' goalkeeper range.

We expect the new team to be available for the kick off of the new season, and I believe it only right that the launch of the team should be at the Chardock Toy Shop with Billy 'Beanpole' Archer and their most notable players present to autograph the new Chardock Subbuteo team.

I have arranged for you to receive a sample of the new team, which I hope you will approve.

All the best for the new season.

Kind regards

Yours sincerely

Trevor A Spencer

CHARDOCK RANGERS FOOTBALL CLUB.THE ALLOTMENTS.CHARDOCK

The Greatest Football Team in the World

West Ham United Supporters Club
Upton Park
London

Dear Sirs,

We've only got 47 supporters.Got any spares ?

Yours faithfully,

Maurice Millionaire
Chardock Rangers Football Club.

West Ham United Supporters Club

(AFFILIATED TO THE NATIONAL FEDERATION OF SUPPORTERS CLUBS)

CASTLE STREET, EAST HAM, LONDON, E.6 Tel: 081-472 1680

Mr Maurice Millionaire,
Chardock Rangers Football Club,
The Allotments,
Chardock
Dorset.

Dear Maurice Millionaire,

No.

Yours faithfully,

Larry Little,
Club Secretary

CHARDOCK RANGERS FOOTBALL CLUB.THE ALLOTMENTS.CHARDOCK

The Greatest Football Team in the World

Kevin King
South Coast Radio

Dear Kevin King,

I am writing to offer you the rights to broadcast our European football matches.I think it would be a great idea ifall your programmes are interrupted by three quarters of an hour for match reports,with some of our players presenting the programmes themselves.Bill Stodge,one of our reserves,is a well experienced orator having spoken at two weddings and once in court presenting his own defence against an unsavoury accusation regarding a couple of farm animals.

Please let me know your availability on Tuesday afternoons next season.

Yours faithfully,

Maurice Millionaire
Chairman and Goons fan
Chardock Rangers Football Club.

15 August 1991

Maurice Millionaire
Chardock Rangers Football Club
The Allotments
Chardock

Dear Maurice

Viva Chardock! We are happy to confirm that South Coast Radio will be delighted to broadcast coverage of Chardock Rangers' bid for European success. The timing of your offer could not have come at a better time as we are currently planning a series of 'Sports Specials'. To date, we have secured the rights to cover Shergar's* return to racing, to be ridden by hitherto unknown jockey, Lord Lucan*, and we are proud to announce exclusive coverage of this year's Inter-Convent Mud Wrestling Championships (Southern Region). Add to that a programme featuring the excitement of inner-city sheep-dog trials, and yes, holding the rights to Chardock's European games will indeed to be glace cherry on the sporting cake!

Sadly, I must decline your offer of star players such as Bill Stodge presenting our programmes as he would have to be a member of *The Association of Lay Entertainers with No Training,* and as the name implies, he would not qualify.

Flattered though I am in you invitation for me to work on Radio Chardock, my contract here is binding (it's an eggslusive!)**. It would have been a wonderful opportunity to make use of my increasing language skills, especially Spanish, although how useful 'es possible apacar mi burrito aqui?' (excuse me, can I park my little donkey here?) would have been I'm not sure.

Notwithstanding these last negative points, we do look forward to discussing the further details of Chardock's rise to (I'm sure) European Supremacy.

Yours sincerely

Kevin King

* subject to availability
** copyright 'The Disc Jockey Handbook 1968'

Radio House, PO Box 2000, Brighton BN41 2SS
Tel: 0273 430111 Fax: 0273 430098

Radio House, Whittle Avenue, Segensworth West, Fareham, Hampshire PO15 5PA
Tel: 0489 589911 Fax: 0489 589453

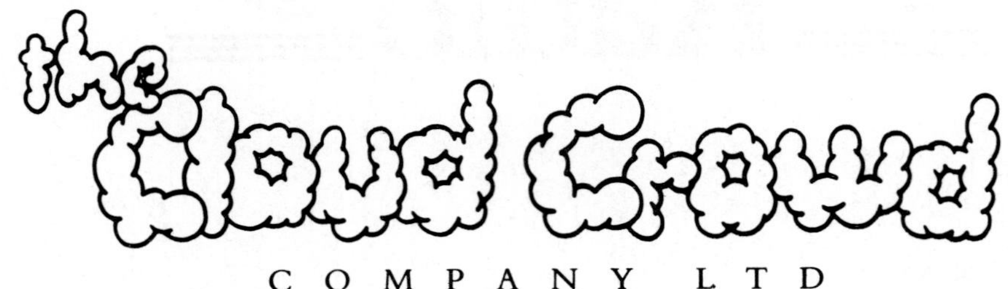

Maurice Millionaire
Chardock Rangers Football Club
The Allotments
Chardock

Dear Mr Millionaire,

In reply to your one and a half hour enquiry this afternoon,left on our answerphone, regarding the possibility of manufacturing and designing fluffy, cuddly toy replicas of your playing staff,after much thought we have decided to pass on the idea.

May we also add that we find it very hard to believe you are in the process of signing Sooty and Sweep as your full backs and three cuddly teddy bears in your midfield

Thank you for your enquiry and we wish you the very best of luck in your project,we feel you may well need it!

Yours faithfully

The Cloud Crowd Ltd

DIRECTORS:
"SOUTH LODGE," 22 LANSDOWNE ROAD, ANGMERING, WEST SUSSEX BN16 4JX. TELEPHONE 0903 771578. FAX 0903 771578
REGISTERED OFFICE NILE HOUSE P.O. BOX 1034 NILE STREET BRIGHTON EAST SUSSEX BN1 1JB REGISTERED COMPANY NO: 2420265

CHARDOCK RANGERS FOOTBALL CLUB.THE ALLOTMENTS.CHARDOCK

The Greatest Football Team in the World

Richard Digance
London Weekend Television.

Dear Richard Digance,

Having exhausted my extensive list of writers for the Chardock club song,I am beginning to fear we must settle for someone desperate for the work.Hence my letter.

Neither Mozart nor the Singing Postman bothered to reply,and neither did Paul McCartney,though I presume he has enough on his plate touring with the Beatles. My request to Elton John was not very tuneful and in bad taste.

Will you please write a version in English and another in foreign.

Yours faithfully,

Maurice Millionaire

Maurice Millionaire
Brass Band leader
Chardock Rangers Football Club.

THE CHARDOCK RANGERS OFFICIAL SONG

Chardock,Chardock
You're always in our hearts,
Even though your players
Are like a bunch of tarts.
They cannot run,they cannot kick
Their Chairman is a proper dick.
Even though it's hard to understand
We think Chardock are the best team in the land.

Chardock,Chardock
They never ever win.
They didn't score one goal last year
And let two hundred in.
But we stand on the terraces,
We sadly lacking few
Shouting Chardock,Chardock,
Chardock Rangers we love you.

Chardock,Chardock,
We don't expect a lot.
We only hope next season
That you have at least one shot!
But win or lose or draw
We Chardock Boys don't care.
Not that we have too much choice
We work for Millionaire

Chardock,Chardock
We think you are the best.
Sod it...no we don't
You're rubbish,we're depressed
Chardock Chardock
You could put us on the map.
Somehow we all doubt it
Chardock you are........
The best team in the Land.

Good Luck!
Richard Digance

Specially composed for Chardock Rangers by RICHARD DIGANCE

CHARDOCK RANGERS OFFICIAL SONG

FOREIGN VERSION

Chardock,Chardock,
Produit de lavage,
Chardock,Chardock,
Devisser le bouchon du reservoir a sel
Mettre l'entonnoir fourni dans
le goulot du reservoir
Chardock,Chardock (Francais)

Chardock,Chardock,
Beim Offnen wahrend des Spulens
Stoppt das Gerat automatische
und lauft nach SchlieBen der Tur
Automatisch wieder
Hohe,Tiuefe,Breite
Chardock,Chardock,(Deutsch)

Chardock,Chardock,
Kapaciteit,12 internationale
standaard couverts.
Netspanning Totaal opgonomen
vermogen.
Toegestane waterdruk
Overige gegevens
Chardock,Chardock,(Nederlands)

Chardock Chardock,
Si el aparato tiene una averia
llamar al Servicio Asistencia
indicando el numero de
Modelo que esta sobre
la tarjeta matricula
Chardock,Chardock(Espanol)

Chardock,Chardock,
We sureendio (Italiano)

CHARDOCK RANGERS FOOTBALL CLUB.THE ALLOTMENTS.CHARDOCK

The Greatest Football Team in the World.

Dickie Davies
Television Presenter
Car Boot Sale
Chardock.

Dear Dickie Davies,

May I offer my congratulations,belated as they may be,on a splendid commentary on Queen Victoria's funeral.My grandad has praised your skills since he was a lad,and I'm writing to invite you to narrate on our first club video.

I recently saw 'Bambi' on video.I don't know if you did all the voices on that,but it was so moving I cried.Perhaps we could create a similar story for Chardock Rangers with yourself playing the part of all the furry animalswith perhaps the inclusion of Rosie,our barmaid, who has the fifth biggest knockers in Europe.
I look forward to your reply.By the way,is Queen Victoria really dead or was that an earlier take ?

Yours faithfully,

Maurice Millionaire
Chardock Rangers Football Club.

Dickie Davies Ltd
Silver Streak House
Warmwelcome Lane
WALLOP Herts

Dear Maurice

I much appreciate the kind things you say about my commentary on Queen Victoria's funeral. It may interest you to know that I refined my technique and my pace watching Cliff Thorburn and Terry Griffiths fight it out over 31 frames. They are to electrifying action what Paul Gascoigne is to the Peace Corps.

Your invitation to narrate, and indeed appear in your video is tempting, particularily as you are using such sophisticated hardware, and, of course because I'd be working closely with Rosie from the Dog and Duck, but I'm already promised to the Wallop Wanderers.

Have you tried Tony Gubba or Kenneth Branagh? - he's an actor, Maurice...

Yours regretfully,

Dickie Davies

Chapter Seven

The Massed Media

Chapter seven.......The Massed Media

I had always maintained an agreement with the BBC whereby they did not televise Chardock's games and I didn't buy their television licence.It was time to change,bite lip,swallow pride,throw gauntlet,honestly the rubbish you go through when admitting you're wrong.

No matter how ugly that girl was who tried to flog us a telly with a fingamebob on it,television was the fulcrum to lever Chardock Rangers towards soccer supremacy,and so twas time to fall in line with those silly adverts,boring programmes about trying to catch criminals,though may I say I bare no personal grudge on that score.Once the rest of the country saw our skills,both here and in Europe,I was convinced they would jam the lanes of Chardock for a glimpse of my eleven athletes.

One night,I flicked through the channels,pausing only to glimpse upon my favourites,noted the names of the television chaps I should contact and proceeded to track them down with the now familiar letter.

I told them all how much I'd enjoyed the 'Lone Ranger' so they knew I wasn't bullshitting,and started laying down,if I may say so myself,some heavy deals to these monied bodies. They would soon be clamouring for film rights,but in the meantime I just sat back enjoying yet another repeat of a 'Carry On' film,admiring Barbara Windsor's stunning pair of full backs.Life seemed so happy when everyone was black and white.You know what I mean.Eastenders is in colour and you couldn't wish top meet a more miserable bunch in your life could you?

Anyway,if I wanted mass media I'd ring the Pope!

CHARDOCK RANGERS FOOTBALL CLUB.THE ALLOTMENTS.CHARDOCK

The Greatest Football Team in the World

Michael Hurll Television
London.

Dear Michael Hurll,

I was given your name by a big star on TV whose name escapes me for the moment.Would you like the European rights of our cup campaign next season.You'll need a long extension lead for away matches and one of those dual purpose sockets you use in hotels for your razor.

I'm afraid I cannot help with fees as I know little on this subject,though I did read once that a bloke in 'Jaws' blaggd a million quid.Well,as there's eleven of us,how about eleven million quid (ten for cash)?

I await your reply.

Yours faithfully,

Maurice Millionaire.

18 July 1991

Maurice Millionaire Esq
Chardock Rangers Football Club
The Allotments
Chardock

Dear Mr Millionaire

RE - CHARDOCK RANGERS

Thank you for your letter which I received today.

Firstly I should point out that Michael Hurll Television is primarily interested in Entertainment programmes not Sport, but judging by your letter you seem to have managed to encompass both.

Perhaps you should think about contacting a network channel like Border or Channel TV, or if you need investment and coverage from abroad, how about Gibraltar TV? At this time of year it is more that likely that the major companies like BBC, NBC, ITV etc have their schedules already allocated. When you approach the networks, you must realise that you will have to convince them 101% that Chardock Rangers Football Club is really worth the kind of coverage you require. It's probably best not to mention money at this stage.

I hope this will be of some help . If you reach the European Cup Finals I'm sure there would be more room for negotiation and if you sign Paul Gascoigne, could you get me his autograph?

Good luck with your venture

Yours sincerely

SUSIE DARK

☐ 6 Brewer Street, London W1R 3SP Tel: 071 465 0103 Fax 071 287 4315
☐ 101 Kingston Hill, Kingston, Surrey KT2 7PZ Tel: 081 549 7005 Fax 081 547 3696
Company Reg. No: 1241877. V.A.T No: 249 4631 41

CHARDOCK RANGERS FOOTBALL CLUB.THE ALLOTMENTS.CHARDOCK

The Greatest Football Team in the World

John Kaye Cooper
London Weekend Television
London.

Dear John Kaye Cooper,

Any chance of staying on air an extra couple of days past the week-end to cover our Tuesday afternoon matches live ?

Yours faithfully,

Maurice Millionaire

Maurice Millionaire
Chairman and Cilla Black fan
Chardock Rangers Football Club.

LONDON WEEKEND TELEVISION LIMITED
THE LONDON TELEVISION CENTRE UPPER GROUND LONDON SE1 9LT
TELEPHONE 071-620 1620

DIRECT LINE: 071-261 3713 DIRECT FAX: 071-261 3228

RC/SJD

15th August 1991

Mr Maurice Millionaire
Chardock Rangers Football Club
The Allotments
Chardock

Dear Maurice Millionaire

Your letter to John Kaye Cooper was passed onto me as he's far too busy to deal with the humdrum of ordinary folk. As you are no doubt aware, JKC is Controller of Entertainment (despite being a Leeds fan) and as well as negotiating multi-million pound deals his duties also include decorating Cilla's dressing room, trimming Beadle's beard and modelling Dame Edna's frocks - although the latter might be for personal enjoyment only.

I'm sorry to have to tell you your request for us to televise Chardock's matches has arrived a little late. Bearing in mind that a Super League seems imminent we have arranged exclusive coverage of Amstrad Social Club Second XI (who now play at White Hart Lane) and the Blind Beggar XI who play in the Mile End Road League. Interesting team this - they always attract huge crowds and yet immediately afterwards most people deny they were at the match and those that admit they were don't remember anything about it (the same as at White Hart Lane in fact).

We might be able to get Danny Baker and Jenni Barnett to do a documentary on the team but to be honest you'd probably get more viewers on Sky.

Can I suggest you try Central TV? They've been looking for something different ever since they stopped making "The Price Is Right" and you might find they'll even throw in Leslie Crowther.

Yours sincerely

ROBIN CARR
EXECUTIVE PRODUCER, COMEDY

THE QUEEN'S AWARD FOR EXPORT ACHIEVEMENT

CHARDOCK RANGERS FOOTBALL CLUB.THE ALLOTMENTS.CHARDOCK

The Greatest Football Team in the World

Publicity Officer
Thames Television
Teddington Lock
Middlesex.

Dear Sirs,

As none of the teams we shall meet in the European Cup next season are on the River Thames,please excuse us for not offering you to bid for the rights to these important games.

However,notwithstanding,may I add this in no way dilutes my interest in being a guest on your 'This Is Your Life' programme when I am available.Get in touch and I'll let you know the rotten pigs I wouldn't have on for love nor money.

Yours faithfully,

Maurice Millionaire
Chardock Rangers Football Club.

Mr Maurice Millionaire
Chardock Rangers Football Club
The Allotments,
Chardock
Dorset

Dear Mr Millionaire,

Your apologies are graciously accepted and we shall be in contact one day regarding the other matter

With best wishes,

Yours sincerely,

Thames Television Plc

THAMES TELEVISION PLC 149 Tottenham Court Road
London
W1P 9LL

Telephone 071-387 9494
Telex 25286

Registered Address 306-316 Euston Road
London NW1 3BB
Registration Number 926655 Registered in England

CHARDOCK RANGERS FOOTBALL CLUB.THE ALLOTMENTS.CHARDOCK

The Greatest Football Team in the World

David Hill
British Sky Broadcasting
Isleworth

Dear David Hill,

Could you please let me know how much more than the BBC and ITV you would be prepared to pay for the exclusive rights of all Chardock Rangers' home fixtures next season ? I feel sure you could sneak in with a better offer while they squabble.

Would you need to send someone along with a camera or would you prefer we did our own film and posted it on sometime ?A godson of mine is fairly keen on films; he has his own photo album now,and I enclose a snap he took in Majorca.I apologise it only shows the sky but he was pissed at the time and flat on his back.

We do not want to play second fiddle to 4th division matches from Bulgaria,even if they are more interesting I could ask the players to shout their names out when they get the ball and then you can dispense with commentators.

I would appreciate a quick reply as I need to get one of those dishes as my wife uses our existing one as a wok when we have friends over.

Yours faithfully,

Maurice Millionaire

Maurice Millionaire
Chardock Rangers Football Club.

BRITISH SKY BROADCASTING

11 October 1991

Maurice Millionaire
Chardock Rangers Football Club
The Allotments
CHARDOCK

Dear Maurice Millionaire

Gosh! There we were, sitting and wondering about how we could make further inroads into the audience of BBC and ITV, when in came your magnificent offer.

The exclusive rights to all Chardock Rangers' home games!

You've obviously seen our advertisements showing that Sky Sports shows football every night of the week, and with your obvious entrepreneurial skills have decided to home in on our rapidly growing market.

Right - you're obviously a man who doesn't like to mess around, so here's the deal.

1. Just get your Godson to take a few snaps of the game, and pop them into any local chemist - who will forward them on to us in the fullness of time.

2. I'd rather not have a commentator - could the players carry large cards which show their name, position and their salary, and when they receive the ball, hold them up in the general direction of your Godson, at the same time shouting out their names.

3. Scheduling such an important fixture will pose some problems, however we could start a special slot at 4am, tenatively being given the working title "Football for Insomniacs" which our scheduling department, after much thought, feel would be an ideal timeframe for Chardock Rangers.

4. Payment will be made in mirrors, axes and beads commensurate with the achieved ratings.

BRITISH SKY BROADCASTING LIMITED
HEAD OFFICE AND REGISTERED OFFICE: 6 CENTAURS BUSINESS PARK, GRANT WAY, ISLEWORTH, MIDDLESEX TW7 5QD
TELEPHONE 071 782 3000 FAX 071 782 3030
REGISTERED IN ENGLAND NO 2247735 VAT REG NO 547 7603 01

We look forward to a long and fruitful relationship, and I'm also forwarding a special copy of "Stir Fry Cooking for Fun and Profit", which I'm sure your wife would appreciate.

Yours in football,

David Hill

D B HILL
Head of Sports
British Sky Broadcasting

HAMPSHIRE COUNTY CRICKET CLUB

Chief Executive:
A.F. BAKER F.C.A.

Marketing Manager:
M.N.S. TAYLOR

COUNTY CRICKET GROUND
NORTHLANDS ROAD
SOUTHAMPTON S09 2TY
Telephone: 0703 - 333788
Fax: 0703 - 330121
Cricketscene
Instant Scores: 0839 - 333366
Reports: 0839 - 333365

Mr.Maurice Millionaire
Chardock Rangers.
The Allotments
Dorset.

Dear Maurice Millionaire,

I've had second thoughts.It's all very well my brother declining the offer from Australia,but to be honest, I didn't realise I'd be playing in the company of Nudger Dixon,Ernie Dredge,and Leonardo Salvador Mario Di Vicente Nasimento,the Nawab of Chardock (How is the old piss head?).

I'd love to play for Chardock Rangers,but bear in mind I was born in South Africa so could you send me a book of rules.I am busy playing cricket in the summer,and in the winter I tour with England,In the Autumn I run a coaching course and in the Spring I go shopping with my wife,but any other time,consider me in!

Look forward to hearing from you,and for obvious reasons I don't give my personal phone number to idiots like you.

Yours sincerely,

Robin Smith
Hampshire and England.

SPONSORED BY
BKL
Brooking Knowles
& Lawrence
Chartered Accountants

CHARDOCK RANGERS FOOTBALL CLUB

THE ALLOTMENTS
CHARDOCK
DORSET

manager:-nudger dixon
chairman:-maurice millionaire

It is with the greatest sadness that I hereby declare,Chardock Rangers Football Club closed down due to lack of interest.

As Club Chairman I have written to all leading European clubs,breaking the sad news,and it makes me a proud man to notice that all the top teams throughout the World are far too shell-shocked and distraught at this news to reply.

I have resigned as Club Chairman and my team manager has returned to school.

This is a day of great sadness and disappointment.In the words of a famous terraces favourite,my dreams simply faded and died.

No press release will be issued.This is the final and binding statement of Chardock Rangers Football Club,the football team that so many said were 'The Greatest Team in The World............'

Oh by the way,the headed notepaper turned up today.

It seems that football at World class level would never be played at Chardock.Now cricket ....that's another story..............

And our additional contributors......

Martin Diplock	Estate Agent.Lyme Regis
Bryan Moore	Chairman.Yeovil Town Football Club.
Mike Keep	Managing Director.Manders Decorative Supplies
Jim French	Commercial Manager.Atcost Buildings.
Dave Courtney	Managing Director.3D Cricket.
Polly Digance	Writer for Nudger Dixon
Tony Williams	Managing Director.Football Directories
Phil Walder	Paper Plane Publishing.
Sean O'Sullivan	Managing Director.Allied Irish Bank
A.Baldrick	Station Master.Axminster Station
Jonathan Haslam	Press Office.10 Downing Street
S.McArthur	Holiday Inn.
Graham Hunter	General Sales Manager.British Midland
Trevor Spencer	Subbuteo Games
Larry Little	West Ham United Supporters Club
Wendy Payne	The Cloud Crowd Ltd.
Michael Hurll	Managing Director.Michael Hurll Services
Robin Carr	Executive Producer.London Weekend Television
Press Office	Thames Television
David Hill	Head of Sport.British Sky Broadcasting